5

THE POWER OF
RELATIONAL EVANGELISM

WAYNE WHITAKER

WESTBOW
PRESS®
A DIVISION OF THOMAS NELSON
& ZONDERVAN

WestBow Press books may be ordered through booksellers or by contacting:

WestBow Press
A Division of Thomas Nelson & Zondervan
1663 Liberty Drive
Bloomington, IN 47403
www.westbowpress.com
1 (866) 928-1240

ISBN: 978-1-5127-1456-2 (sc)
ISBN: 978-1-5127-1457-9 (hc)
ISBN: 978-1-5127-1464-7 (e)

Library of Congress Control Number: 2015916156

Print information available on the last page.

WestBow Press rev. date: 10/08/2015

To Wendy, Zachary, Colby, and Anna Catherine.
You are my life, love, and inspiration. And,
to my parents whose faith stories inspired my own.

Contents

Preface

Evangelism—a word that strikes fear in the hearts of many Christians. I'm not saying that Christians don't see its universal importance. In fact, if you were to ask true believers about the importance of sharing one's faith with others, I'm sure most would agree that evangelism is one of the chief, if not the most important, functions and responsibilities of the church. The stark reality, however, is that while most Christians are quick to acknowledge the importance of evangelism, surprisingly few actually involve themselves in the endeavor.

In a December 2013 article, the Barna Group pointed out that though 73% of born again Christians believe that there is an individual responsibility to share one's faith with others, only 52% had actually done so at least once in the past year. These numbers are a bit higher among evangelicals. However, even among this group, one-third who believe they have a personal responsibility to share still have not done so.[i]

Why, if we all agree that sharing our faith stories is so important, are so few of us actually doing it? I believe that there are a few reasons for this. Let me first say that I don't believe we can simply make the assumption that Christians don't care about lost people anymore! In fact, I believe that many people's experiences may mirror my own.

Perhaps their refusal to share is grounded in an overwhelming sense of inadequacy for the task rather than a lack of true conviction.

I came to faith in Christ as a seven-year-old child during the 1980's. At that time, there was a strong emphasis on evangelism, missions, and outreach in the American church. However, I was like many others during that time: after praying to receive Christ, not much else happened for me. While I was convinced of my need for Jesus, I wasn't immediately taught that my new faith story was part of a greater story of redemption meant for all mankind. Specifically, I wasn't taught that I had a personal responsibility to take the message of the gospel to a lost world. While I was discipled strongly in all the things I *shouldn't* do as a believer, there wasn't nearly as much emphasis on the things I *should* do…other than praying, reading my Bible, and going to church. Therefore, my responsibility for sharing Christ totally escaped me during the formative years of my faith.

My experience growing up in church was one in which I saw myself as a civilian Christian while pastors, evangelists, and missionaries were the *real* soul winners. In fact, I came to believe that the best thing I could do was leave heavy things like evangelism to the professionals. Years later, as I grew more mature in the faith (actually *after* I got to seminary), I realized that every Christian was meant to be a soul winner. To my surprise I learned this task was precisely why Jesus left His church here in the first place…to make disciples and to spread the gospel. With this new realization came the conviction that it was high time for me to start doing something about reaching the lost. There was only one problem: I didn't know how to share my faith! Since the soul winners I had been exposed to were pastors, evangelists, and missionaries, I assumed that I needed the proper training before I could really get serious about telling others about Jesus.

During my seminary years, I committed myself to gathering all the needed resources to ensure that I could do my part as an effective soul winner for God's kingdom. Of course, it helped that evangelism and missions classes were a mandatory part of my degree program. The passion that I developed for sharing the gospel during those years was amazing. I sat at the feet of godly men whom I considered to be modern day heroes of the faith and whose passion for the gospel was contagious! To be honest, the convictions birthed in me during those years have shaped every part of my life and ministry since. Everything wasn't perfect, however.

As far as I was concerned, seminary was a somewhat clinical experience; consequently, I came away from seminary with some misconceptions about leading people to Jesus. My heroes in the area of evangelism were guys who could sit down on a plane and talk to just about anyone about Jesus, often successfully leading that person to the Lord. These were guys who had no qualms with walking up to complete strangers and dynamically sharing their faith in a way that convinced others of a need for Jesus. While it is clear to me now that these men had a spiritual gift of evangelism, I began to think that this was the only correct approach. I remember how this played out in my life.

I had a close friend in seminary who was also passionate about evangelism. Each week we played golf at a local course. Golf, of course, is a prerequisite to pastoral ministry, correct? As students, we couldn't afford a cart, so we walked the course. As we walked, we made it our goal to find another player to join us, hoping that we might be able to share the gospel. Our plan was to share a tract and hopefully see a person come to Christ each week. While this was a noble idea, the thought never crossed our minds that two guys tag-teaming to present a canned presentation would come across as nothing less than awkward to a complete stranger. It didn't help that the inherent time constraint of the whole plan meant that we felt a very real pressure to push someone towards making a decision right there in the midst of his bogeys and birdies! We had quite a few spirited conversations with people, but I can't honestly tell you of one single person who came to faith through our efforts. Looking back on all of these attempts, I now realize that I had a great understanding of the nuts and bolts of evangelism but was completely missing out on the relational aspect of the whole thing.

During this time in my spiritual development, I read book after book on the topic of evangelism. I learned the Four Spiritual Laws and studied one presentation after another in order to perfect *how* to lead others to Christ. I studied apologetics so I would have answers to any questions I might be asked. I honed my approach and looked for opportunities to practice my craft. Anytime I had the opportunity to share with someone, I treated it almost as if I were making a sales pitch. After all, that approach was how many of the presentations I had learned sounded to me. The process of leading someone to saving faith became more like leading someone through a flow chart or selling a car than introducing them to another person, let alone the God of the universe. I would lead folks in the "sinner's prayer," dogmatically making sure that every word was said correctly as if the ABCs of becoming a Christian were a formula to be followed to the letter. I seriously believed that if someone left out the word "admit" I needed to make him pray the prayer all over again. I learned the Romans Road by heart and felt prepared to handle any situation, answer any question, and convince anyone of his need for Christ.

Now, let me share a part of my story that I'm not at all proud of: I kept a tally of people I led to the Lord. Just as a flying ace in World War I might make a mark on his plane for each enemy he shot down in battle, I kept a mental tally of every person I led to the Lord. I don't know why I did this, but I'm pretty sure it was a pride thing. Maybe I was thinking that I would be able to stand before Jesus one day and give Him a list of all the people I had led to Him — as if I really had anything to do with their salvation, or as if my service made me any more or less valuable to His kingdom! The truth is that for all my training in evangelism, I was still very immature. At that point in my faith development, evangelism was really about trying to prove my worth or proficiency as a believer. I didn't grasp the depth of love that the gospel story was meant to convey. I had institutionalized the whole process and found a way to present the cold, hard facts without the messiness of actually relating to the people with whom I shared. Of course, it goes without saying that I took no responsibility for the continued growth of these people once they "prayed the prayer." In my mind, once someone prayed to accept Christ, I had done my job!

This lack of relationality in my approach meant that as I shared the gospel with people, I was very professional and almost business-like. I rarely shared my own testimony because, at least in my mind, there was nothing exciting about a seven-year-old boy realizing his need for Christ simply because he watched his parents model *their* need for Christ. I faithfully shared the nuts and bolts of the gospel, but missed out on the most important part: *connecting through relationships*! I tended to keep things impersonal, preferring not to share my own struggles or the work Christ was doing in my own life. It's almost as if I tried to convince others of their need for Jesus without revealing to them that my need for Jesus was just as great.

At some point I lost count of the number of people I led to Christ. To be honest, I've wondered over the years how many of those were true converts anyway. I'm afraid that my flawed view of evangelism led to an equally flawed understanding of their coming to Jesus. I felt like I was fulfilling a contractual obligation to share the gospel similar to a car salesman's trying to close a deal. Sometimes I wonder how many of the people I talked to bought into the presentation instead of the Savior behind it. In other words, it's completely possible that some of those relied on a perfectly worded prayer rather than a relationship with the One to whom they were praying for salvation. The point here is that I boiled evangelism down to a religious activity when the truth of the gospel and the power of the Great Commission lie in their inherent relationality.

I did with evangelism what a lot of us want to do with many things in the Christian world. We love to condense things down to programs and procedures. This practice is nothing new. If you've been in church culture very long, I'm sure you've noticed that any time a church starts something new and successful other churches want to know how to package and implement the idea so they too can experience growth. In fact, some megachurches will even hold conferences to teach others how to implement their ministry structure within their own church context. While this isn't always bad, we often forget that some things are successful only because of the atmosphere in which they exist. In other words, the personality of the church, its relationship with the community, and the relationships of believers within that particular church determine what kinds of things work for a church. The truth is that no single program or process will work in all places because church life involves people and is, therefore, inherently relational. The same is true of evangelism.

In my pursuit to become a better evangelist, I sought out programs and processes I could lead people through expecting that these would apply to all people at all times and in all places. The fact of the matter is that no such *program* exists. Why? Because, just like in church life, evangelism is about people; specifically it's about introducing people to the greatest *Someone* they could ever meet. As such, evangelism is, at the very heart of its being, tied to intimate relationship.

An evolution in my understanding of what evangelism truly is has given rise to the writing of this book. As I've realized the relationality of evangelism, it's become more and more apparent that a cookie-cutter approach to leading people to the God of the universe can't work. Just as no one eyeglass prescription is correct for all who need clearer vision, so no one evangelistic prescription will work for all who need spiritual vision. Now, let me be clear about something: everyone who comes to the Father must do so through His Son, Jesus. I'm *not* saying that there are many different ways to God— that's religious pluralism. The combination of Christ's redeeming work on the cross and our faith in Him as Lord and Savior is the only thing that will save us. Jesus makes this clear in John 14:6 when He emphatically states that He alone is "the way, the truth, and the life." No one gets to the Father unless they go through Him. The fact remains, however, that though each of us must go through the same narrow door of Jesus, we each arrive at that door in a little different way.

It's often been said, "Christ meets people where they are." The problem with a "one-size fits all" concept of evangelism is that it doesn't take the individual needs of people into consideration. In the field of education, there have been great leaps in understanding that each child is an individual learner with his own personal learning style. One of my own children has what's called an IEP (Individualized Education Plan) because his method of learning is radically different from that of his peers. Every part of his education is tailored to his specific needs. This approach to learning has proven very successful in helping him to reach some pretty lofty goals. The world of education has come to realize that every child is different; thus, every child's education must be a little different. Just as educational needs are individual, so are people's life stories, contexts, backgrounds, and immediate needs. If we want to be truly successful in leading others to faith in Christ, we must discover a way of doing so that takes into account their unique situations, allowing us to individualize our approaches. Therefore, effective evangelism must simultaneously be relational and individual.

These two facts lead to one inescapable conclusion: what we need in today's church culture is an understanding of how to approach evangelism with an eye towards individual needs and relationships rather than through a program or planned out process. Such an approach to evangelism must be both relational and customizable so that it is capable of being individualized. What would make this approach even greater is if it could also incorporate a low-pressure, stress-free vehicle of delivery that would release the presenter of the gospel from feeling like he needs to have all the answers or that he must "close the deal" immediately. The amazing fact is that the perfect tool for this type of approach already exists! In fact, we see it used in Scripture over and over again. Jesus used this approach as well as Paul, Peter, Luke, John, and others. Furthermore, we use this same tool daily in the world of business, family, entertainment, and education. The tool I'm referring to is *conversation*!

As people of faith, we need to learn how to incorporate faith issues into normal everyday conversations with people in a way that helps us to come across as real, all the while taking the "pushiness" out of evangelism. If we could learn to have spiritual conversations with people or, more importantly, if we knew how to turn any conversation in a spiritual direction, think about how much easier it would be to share the gospel. Think about how it might take the fear out of evangelism if we were to learn how to gauge where the Spirit of God is at work, joining in alongside Him rather than attempting to work *for* Him. How much easier would it be to do this within the context of relationships where a measure of trust and caring has already been established? Imagine how much more enjoyable it would be to approach every opportunity from a relational standpoint, taking into account the individual rather than implementing a canned program or pitch. What if we had a set of tools that allowed us to work within the fluidity of conversation and the give-and-take of everyday relationships to share our faith stories?

I love to work with wood. I have built things as large as buildings and as small as bird houses. Regardless of the project, I always approach the job with a core set of tools in my bag: a tape measure, a hammer, a saw, a square, a sander, and some type of fastener. This core set of tools allows me to handle any challenge that may arise during the project. What if we had a set of tools for evangelism that would allow us to approach situations from various perspectives with confidence. Having these tools would allow us to make use of them as God directs, guiding the flow of conversation in a spiritual direction with a set goal in mind.

In order for us to approach the idea of evangelism from this perspective or, more accurately, in order for us to get back to the heart of evangelism as it is demonstrated in God's Word, we need to identify the tools which will help us begin to think correctly about this concept of relational evangelism. This book will focus on "5 sets of 5" which are meant to help believers form a biblical way of thinking about evangelism and provide tools needed to challenge them to fulfill the task. These tools assist us in leveraging the power of conversations and relationships to the greatest extent for the purpose of sharing our faith. In this book, the reader will discover the following:

1. 5 biblical and relational reasons Christians must be passionate about sharing the gospel
2. 5 things Christians can pray on a daily basis to pave the way for spiritual conversations
3. 5 questions that can be asked in the context of any conversation to determine the present spiritual condition of another person
4. 5 passages that succinctly explain the gospel
5. 5 responses one might expect and how to handle each one in a way that promotes further conversation

As we uncover these tools, I'll remind you that there is no set timetable for leading someone to faith in Christ. There is no need to feel like we must make all of this happen in one sitting; nor is there a reason to pressure anyone. We should remember that the work of salvation is the domain of God. It is the Holy Spirit of God, Himself, who convinces a person of his need for Christ, quickens his heart to understanding, and communicates through us to make His truth known. As such, we are simply following His lead and allowing Him to use these tools through us to create opportunities. All of this requires that we grasp the concept of having *ongoing* spiritual conversations with people, creating an atmosphere in which others have the freedom to discover and grow to Christ.

The approach to evangelism discussed in this book is the culmination of lessons I've learned through my years of ministry within the church, specifically among young people. It comes out of a maturing process of my own understanding of the relationality of the message of the gospel. It takes into account the individuality of personhood and leverages the power of the human element in communication. It arises out of a desire to help God's people realize that He has already given them every tool they need to take the gospel to the "ends of the earth."

I pray that through the pages of this book you will be encouraged. I pray that you will realize the power for salvation that is available to all who believe in Jesus Christ. I pray that you will understand that God is already at work and that He desires for you to join Him. I pray that you will experience the joy that comes from seeing others brought to Christ through your willingness to simply make yourself available. And, I pray that this book inspires you, just as its contents have inspired me, to leverage every single relationship you have for the spread of the gospel, the growth of God's kingdom, and the good of those with whom you share.

First Things First

I absolutely love sure things, and I'm pretty sure that you do as well. Especially when it comes to something that is good or needed, we love to *know* that we can count on things happening just as they are predicted. We feel better about a decision or an investment when we are confident of the outcome.

A perfect example of this is the calm peace we have knowing that things we purchase carry a great warranty. Let's be honest, if you had the choice between two identical items and one was covered by a warranty and the other one not, which would you choose? I'm sure that if you're the least bit logical in your approach to purchases, you would acquire the one with a warranty. Why? Because the warranty provides you with a surety that what you have purchased will still be around in working order when you need it. And if by some chance it's not, you know that the manufacturer will return it to working order. A warranty is a promise, and a promise means that your purchase is a sure thing.

Another example of this—at least for me—shows up when it comes to spending money. I only want to invest my hard-earned money in things that have a guaranteed outcome. I've never been too heavily involved with the stock market for just this reason. In fact, if you were to look at my retirement portfolio, you would discover that almost all my money is invested in mutual funds or companies with long track records of success. I've just never been a gambler when it comes to important resources.

You may be a little more of a risk taker when it comes to these areas, but I'm pretty sure that there are situations in your life where you crave assurances. Why? Because all of us, regardless of who we are, love a sure thing. We each have areas in our lives which we prefer not to leave to chance. We prefer investing our money in things that are sure to return a profit. We prefer purchasing items that are sure to fulfill the needs for which they were acquired. We willingly pour ourselves into relationships that we believe are sure to last. We love having people in our lives who are sure to come through for us when everything else falls apart. We crave entertainment that delivers on its promises. We want our favorite sports teams to win every game. We love a sure thing!

While there are many beautiful and appealing aspects of the gospel message, one of the greatest is the surety of it. We can *know* Christ came to redeem us. We can *know* He paid the price for our sin. We can *know* He is alive and that He reigns. We can *know* that we have salvation. We can *know* that God is trustworthy to forgive and restore those of us who respond to His gift of grace. We can *know* that He is faithful to us even if or when we aren't faithful to Him. How can we know this? Well, look at something that Paul writes in one of his letters.

COVENANT

The letter to the Romans is a treatise on the gospel that Paul proclaimed. In writing to the folks at Rome, Paul systematically explains the gospel message and shares with them how they might have a saving faith that is transformative and eternal. He succinctly lays out the unregenerate state of all mankind as hopeless sinners and illustrates that no man will attain a right relationship with God through religious activities or good works. He portrays Christ as the one and only source of salvation for mankind, sacrificed at the will of the Father for rebellious and sinful people, and made alive through the powerful working of the Spirit of God. He establishes the fact that salvation is based purely in the work of Jesus Christ and is available to all mankind when people place their faith in Him and acknowledge Him as Lord. Perhaps one of the greatest passages in this whole letter pertaining to the surety of faith comes in Romans 10:13. It's here that we read the promise that "whoever calls upon the name of the Lord will be saved." Did you catch the beauty of that statement?

There is one word in Paul's statement that should inspire exuberance in us all! Notice that Paul doesn't say there is a *possibility* for salvation when we call on the Lord. He doesn't portend that we can *earn* salvation through some type of sacrifice or by hard labor. Neither does Paul lead us to believe that salvation is a temporary state founded somehow upon God's faithfulness but dependent in the long-run on our ability to follow through. This murderer turned missionary makes a proclamation here that is both glorious and completely grace inspired. Those who call on Jesus for salvation, regardless of who they may be, *WILL* be saved! God is ready and willing to save anyone who calls on the name of Jesus! He is faithful to fulfill His promise if we will only take Him up on it.

I remember a time that one of my children had climbed a tree and was too afraid to come down. There I stood under him, the faithful father ready to rescue my child, beckoning for him to simply jump and trust that I would catch him. Of course, he had his reservations. He thought that I might drop him. He wasn't sure that I would follow through with my promise. Yet, had he known my heart and the depth of love I held for him, he would have realized that there was no way his loving father would allow a child of his own who had

3

called upon his name for rescue to fall. When he finally worked up the faith to trust me and commit himself to my hands, he found that he had nothing to fear. Regardless of his lack of faith, my willingness to rescue never faltered. My desire to save him did not increase along with the measure of trust he placed in me. Just as he had no need to fear initially, there was no point during this episode at which I suddenly changed my mind or decided he wasn't worthy of saving. Furthermore, I did not expect him, after having jumped into my arms, to somehow earn the right to stay there.

This is a perfect illustration of our relationship to our heavenly Father. When we cast ourselves upon His mercies, He is quick to rescue and sure to save. This is not a relationship that begins with grace but is somehow maintained through works. Paul is abundantly clear—everyone who calls on the name of the Lord *will* be saved! The same grace and mercy that saves us continually sustains us in our relationship with the Father. What an amazing universal truth! We can know with certainty that God the Father will stand by His promise to save, no matter what, when we call on the name of His Son in faith! God's promise is a covenant solidified and perfected by His very character.

I have stated previously that there is no process through which we can lead someone that will result in his salvation. You see, true salvation does not come about through man-made programs or by jumping through a set of religious hoops. It comes only through a relationship with the person of Jesus. To be sure, God has established a plan for making His gracious gift available to mankind. Paul illustrates this fact in the verses following God's promise to save:

> "But how can they call on Him they have not believed
> in? And how can they believe without hearing about
> Him? And how can they hear without a preacher?
> And how can they preach unless they are sent? As it

is written: 'How beautiful are the feet of those who announce the gospel of good things!'"[ii]

Notice the progression here. Paul actually begins in verse thirteen with the act of faith that takes place in calling on Jesus for salvation. In verse fourteen, he begins to work backwards from that decision to reveal the steps that lead up to this result. As we've already discovered, God has the final role to play in this process as He faithfully steps in and grants forgiveness and salvation to all who call upon the name of Jesus in faith. There are, however, a couple of steps leading up to God's faithful response that are dependent upon the actions of the person who is making a decision to place his faith in Christ. In addition, there are initial steps that are wholly and completely dependent upon the faithfulness of believers to share the message of the gospel with those who haven't heard.

CONVICTION

Paul actually begins with a person's exercise of faith in Christ and works backwards from there to give us a better understanding of the important steps that must happen in order for a person to come to believe in Jesus. The first thing that Paul addresses in this passage is actually the last step in the faith process. In order for someone to call upon the name of Jesus, Paul tells us that this person must believe that Christ is who He says He is. The writer of Hebrews states this truth in the following way: "Now without faith it is impossible to please God, for the one who draws near to Him must believe that He exists and rewards those who seek Him."[iii] If people want God to respond with forgiveness and redemption, they must move past a simple assumption of truth to demonstrating a willingness to stake their very lives and eternal futures upon the words of Jesus. In other words, they must come to God with a conviction that they are who He says they are, that He is who He says He is, and that He has done for them what He claims to have done. This conviction is prerequisite to saving faith.

Before anyone can believe in faith, he must first have an opportunity and exhibit a willingness to "hear" the message of the gospel. When Paul uses the word "hear," he isn't simply stating that all anyone needs to do is physically hear the message of Christ. Rather, his point is that if they never hear the message in the first place, they do not have the opportunity to do anything deeper with the information. The fact is that there is hearing, and then there is *hearing*. Jesus loved to follow up His teachings by saying things like "If anyone has ears to hear, let him *hear*." In doing so, Jesus infers that there is more to hearing than just a physical process. Really listening, accepting, and applying His words are prerequisites to believing His message. Paul and Jesus used one word for both the physical act of hearing and the cognitive process of application. In today's language, however, we often make a distinction between the act of hearing and actually listening. While hearing is something that one does automatically, listening is an active pursuit requiring understanding and cognitive involvement. Children illustrate this fact perfectly on a daily basis.

My children often get involved in a television program or video game and completely ignore the requests of their mother or me to come to dinner, get ready for bed, or leave for school. Their excuse is almost always to say, "I didn't hear you when you told me to do that." If you're a parent, I'm sure you've been the recipient of just such a claim. What you and I know to be true, however, is that our children *hear* us just fine but refuse to give us their attention because they aren't actually *listening*. When Paul states that "hearing" the gospel message is prerequisite to believing, he isn't just stating that we need to passively hear its truth. He is saying that we must actively attend to and consider its claims as well.

Therefore, people must not only hear, but must also listen to the message of the gospel if they are to be drawn towards salvation through it. The harsh truth is that some have calloused their hearts and shut their ears to the truth of the gospel of Jesus, refusing its powerful meaning. Perhaps they are unwilling to undergo the change which they know will come as part of a relationship with Christ. Maybe it all seems too good to be true. Some have been convinced by a secular mindset that they have no need for a spiritual Savior, instead believing that Christianity is just another mystical attempt at finding inner peace. Quite possibly, these may even see Christians as weak-minded individuals who are incapable of coping with the reality of the world as it is. Whatever the reason, they never believe in Christ because they have consciously chosen not to listen to the message of Christ. Clearly, this is their decision. You and I can do nothing to force someone to respond to the gospel. All we can do is ensure that the message is made available and that people have the opportunity to hear.

As people actively attend to the truth of the gospel, the Holy Spirit brings about conviction of sin and their need for a Savior. It is this conviction that gives birth to saving faith and the confession of Jesus as Lord. And, here stands another promise: though not all will listen to the message of the gospel, we have the assurance that *some* will. It is a sure thing that if we spread the gospel seed far enough and wide enough, a harvest will be had!

CONNECTION

We've spent a considerable amount of time discussing what it means to really *listen* to the gospel. Let's take a step back and talk about an aspect of "hearing" pertaining to its availability. There are countless millions who would listen and respond to the message of the gospel, yet have never *heard* its truth. While we have no control over who will listen, we have every bit of control over who will hear. In fact, the responsibility to connect lost souls with the truth of Jesus' atoning work falls squarely upon the shoulders of believers. As ambassadors, we seek to connect a dark, dying, and sinful world to a loving, merciful, and gracious God.

According to recent statistics by the global research arm of the Southern Baptist International Mission Board, more than four billion people in this world are members of people groups that have less than a two percent evangelical presence.[iv] That means that the majority of these people will be born, live their lives, and die never having heard the truth that Jesus Christ came to save them. Now, before we assume that this is an issue that only exists in some other part of the world, let me point out that even within our own culture it is becoming increasingly possible for a person to be born into a non-believing home, grow up with non-believing friends, spend days with non-believing co-workers, marry a non-believing spouse, and die without ever having someone personally share with him the amazing truth of the grace and mercy of Jesus.

In the past couple of years, I've developed quite a taste for bluegrass music. This was not a genre to which I had much exposure growing up. In recent years, however, my family has spent a considerable amount of time in the mountains of east Tennessee. I initially came across bluegrass in some of our visits to areas where the music found its roots. As I *heard* the music, I began to develop a liking for it. This led me to *listen* to the music. As I listened, I found that much of the music is deeply spiritual, founded in a practical application of many Biblical truths. The more I *listened,* the more I fell in love with the genre itself. So, let me ask...what came first, the hearing or the listening? Obviously, I had to hear the music before I could ever listen to it. This is precisely the position we find many people in when it comes to the message of Christ. They would listen if they could but *hear* its wonderful truth. The sad truth is that most will never hear the gospel if we don't share it!

There are very few people with whom I have a close relationship that I met on my own. Maybe you're an extrovert who never meets a stranger, but that definitely does not describe me! Almost all my close relationships came about through introductions of mutual friends. In fact, I have cultivated much closer relationships with people that I now call friends than I had with some of the folks who initially introduced me to them. The same is true of a relationship with Christ. If you're a believer, I'm sure that you can identify someone who introduced you to Christ as well, be it a friend, family member, or pastor. We all come to Jesus through relationships with other people. This is the relational aspect that we must never attempt to divorce from our acts of evangelism. When it comes to the salvation experience, it's almost always predicated upon some idea of mutual friendship.

I believe that it's precisely the programmatic nature inherent in many evangelistic strategies that leads to failures. In my years of ministry, I've learned many different programs for evangelism. One thing I found to be true of nearly all of them is that it's very easy to work the program without ever truly developing a relationship with the people we're trying to reach. This leads to an impression of believers as inauthentic, unfriendly, and bigoted. When people believe that we see them as objects to be obtained or prizes to be won, they doubt, for good reason, our motives and our message! True evangelism is by nature relational. It happens as we who are connected to the Father through the power of the Holy Spirit and the work of Christ connect with others, all the while demonstrating intentional love and true fellowship.

As we introduce people to Jesus, we must do all we can to help them foster a great relationship with Jesus. My parents were the ones who introduced me to Christ; however, my relationship with Jesus has grown to be infinitely more important and exponentially deeper than my relationship with them. My wife and I have introduced our children to Jesus, but I assure you that we will feel like failures if their individual relationships with Him don't grow to eclipse all others they have, including the relationships they have with us. We all recognize the emotional, psychological, and social need we have to be and feel connected to others. What we must never forget, however, is that the most important connection that any person could have is with his Creator.

Paul makes it clear that people will never hear or believe if someone doesn't "preach" the good news. I know that this term is heavily loaded with meaning in today's church culture. As a youth pastor, I "preach" on a regular basis; however, the preaching that I do isn't necessarily what Paul refers to here. When you and I hear the word "preach," we immediately contextualize it within modern day American church life, leading many of us to give ourselves an out on sharing the gospel. Our argument is that since we aren't all called to be vocational *preachers,* then neither are we all called to *preach.* This concept has led to the mentality that professional Christians like pastors and missionaries have been given the job of evangelizing, making disciples, and growing the kingdom of God while regular, everyday people of the church only have responsibilities to show up, give their money to support the endeavor, and pray for the success of the *real* ministers. Lets remember one thing, however: when Paul wrote of the need for someone to "preach," he did not have our current use of the term in mind.

While the office of "overseer," the equivalent of a modern-day pastor, was definitely a part of the New Testament church world, Paul uses terminology here that is much more focussed on an act rather than an office. The letter to the Romans was originally written in Greek. As is often the case when translating, one single word doesn't always convey all nuances of the equivalent word in the original language. This is just such a case. The terms Paul uses which are translated "preacher" in verse fourteen and "preach" in verse fifteen share the same root. "Kērūssō" is the *act* of proclaiming or making known good news. While this word is often translated "preach," it is more precisely understood to mean "proclaim good news" or "herald good news." In other words, its use has little to do with an office in the church, but rather the *message* of the church! Paul is making an adamant case, not that we need more pastors sermonizing from pulpits, but that we need more Christians sharing the good news out in the streets! And…let us be clear…this proclamation is the responsibility of every believer!

You know, you and I talk about the things we love. In fact, when we are excited about good news, it's almost impossible to get us to stop talking about it. I've stood in awe many times throughout the years, listening to men and boys accurately recall exact statistics concerning their favorite athletes or teams. Some of you know right this moment who won the Super Bowl in 1988. If you aren't sure about this information yourself, I'm positive that you know exactly who to ask! I've listened as people strike up conversations with complete strangers, carrying on for great amounts of time without ever feeling ashamed or inadequate about issues that excite them. I've witnessed grandparents talk about their grandchildren to absolutely anyone who will listen, sharing a plethora of facts that only they could get excited about. I've also been told by some of these same folks that they feel inadequate to share their faith, or that they find it nearly impossible to memorize Scripture, or that they just don't know how to bring up the gospel. The truth is that we find it easy to talk about the things we love! The obvious questions are "Do we love Christ?" and "Are we thankful for what He's done for us?"

Is it possible that the reason we don't faithfully proclaim the good news of Christ is because we don't truly understand how *good* the news is? Perhaps we don't get excited over the opportunity to be heralds of this great gift because we don't fully understand the depths of our own depravity and the amazing grace offered to us in Christ! If you have experienced the grace of Jesus, then you have been made a recipient of the most amazing act of mercy in all of history. Paul's point is that the only way folks in this world will ever hear about and respond to this great love is if those who have experienced it excitedly proclaim its wonder and splendor!

You see, as people who have been connected to God the Father through His Son Jesus, it is a great responsibility and privilege to join Him in connecting others. Each of us who believe has an amazing faith story that is saturated in the love and grace of the Father. How could we possibly keep this to ourselves? Paul goes on to illustrate the beauty of sharing by exclaiming, "How welcome are the feet of those who announce the gospel of good things!"[v] When you and I participate in the proclamation of the good news of Christ, we are embarking on the greatest endeavor possible.

CONCLUSION

The gospel of Jesus is a sure thing! The plan that God has put into place for the salvation of the world is remarkable. Those who are willing to invest themselves in the kingdom of God will find an everlasting return on their investment. The promises of God are true and trustworthy, and there is no doubt that God will save those who call upon the name of Jesus in faith. He is faithful to hold up His end of the deal.

The fact is that if we will be faithful to share, some will believe! While not everyone who is exposed to the good news of Jesus will respond in faith, we are promised that some will hear the message and be convicted of their need for Christ as their Savior. Of course, that is a decision that squarely falls upon the shoulders of each individual. The sad truth, however, is that many in this world have not had the opportunity to make such a decision because no one has ever shared the gospel message with them. It should devastate us to think that there are many who will experience judgment who could be saved if Christians would do the job given to them.

It is our responsibility and great honor to be used by God in connecting others to Him. As we grow in our relationship with Christ, He helps us to see every other relationship He's put in our lives as an opportunity to share Him with others. And, when we begin to leverage every relationship for the kingdom of God, our approach to evangelism is authentic and laced with love rather than canned, dry, and unfeeling. As we grow to understand that evangelism is truly about people rather than programs, we begin to see that our individual faith stories are part of a greater narrative of God's unfolding story of love, mercy, and grace.

It's helpful to envision the plan that Paul illustrates here as a chain. The hook on each end involves connection. Our connection to God stands on one end while His faithful willingness to connect with others waits on the other. The links between the two involve the hearing and response of the individual as well as the faithful proclamation of God's people. While you and I can do nothing to force others to believe in Christ, we can in essence condemn them for eternity by not making the message of Christ available to them in the first place. You see, you and I are the only possible weak links in this chain.

It's my hope and prayer that God's people will faithfully join in the joyful proclamation of the good news that Christ has come to save us. I'm confident that as you move through the pages of this book, you will be offered tools that will build upon the foundation laid here. As you explore these topics, don't be tempted to think this is just another program. I'm simply offering possible ways to approach the idea of evangelism. Some of these ideas may seem new to you. Most of them will appear very common sensical. None involve a program! In fact, what I suggest will only work in the context of authentic relationships. These are not steps to go through, but rather tools to use. My heart's desire is to see God's people realize that evangelism is not an art form reserved for a precious few Christians, but an active pursuit in which every believer may joyfully be involved.

Are you ready to go? I hope so! Let's jump in to the first 5.

5

Reasons to Share

Let's be honest about something—sharing our faith is rarely easy. Opportunities seem to come at awkward moments. We often feel as though we're stepping out onto a shaky limb when we try to share our faith. Sometimes people are less than receptive, and, yes, that's an understatement! Quite honestly, we're frequently afraid of the consequences. If the opportunity arises at work, we ask ourselves if there's a chance sharing could get us fired. If the opportunity arises at school, we ask ourselves if there's a chance sharing could ruin our reputation. If the opportunity arises at the grocery store, we ask ourselves if there's a chance we could be followed out to the car and have our heads bashed in. Oh, yeah, and what if something we say offends other people? What if others don't agree with our Christian lifestyle? What if they're members of another religion? What if they ask a question for which we don't have an answer? What if, what if, what if?

Well, first of all, let me remind you that this book is all about a relational approach to sharing your faith story. In other words, you will attempt to leverage existing relationships for the gospel, or you will attempt to build new relationships with an eye towards sharing your faith story later on. The point of this is that you don't always have to feel like you *must* lead off in a relationship by saying something like "Hey, are you saved? Because if you're not, you're going to hell!" Don't get me wrong, God will give you opportunities in life in which someone is so close to calling on Him that it feels like ripe pickings. However, most of the time, that situation is not the case. And, you don't need to feel like you have to have all the answers. You need not feel like someone has to agree with you on everything or that you must immediately convince them to see things your way.

If, during the course of talking to someone, you feel that he is searching for God and is ready to make a decision for Christ, by all means lead him to do so. However, if one isn't ready to make such a decision, don't force the issue. The beauty of the approach I am suggesting is that it capitalizes on relationships as a tool by which God can work through you. You will constantly try to build bridges that allow you to have spiritual conversations with people. Just as importantly, you will do everything you can to protect these bridges so that ongoing conversations can take place. That means you'll move along at different paces with people as to when and how often you bring up your own faith story.

I really hope you catch the conversational idea inherent in this. The primary thing we try to do through this approach to evangelism is create opportunities for *spiritual conversations* rather than presentations. Honestly, this one fact should be enough to take most of the tension and anxiety out of sharing your faith. If you can begin to couch spiritual conversations within the normal ebb and flow of the lives of your relationships, you'll find sharing your faith story becomes much simpler. If I just talk to people about who I am and what I believe, I come across as much more authentic than if I am constantly trying to argue, convince, and win them over. So, let's get it straight in our minds right now that we're looking to accomplish spiritual conversations, not presentations. What's the difference?

Conversations are dynamic. There's give and take. When I have a conversation with someone, there is flow. I don't try to manage that flow; I just go with it. There are even times that a conversation will leave one topic and move to another only to come back to the former at a later time. Conversation doesn't involve arguing! In fact, the moment an argument starts, conversation comes to a screeching halt. Arguments tend to be wars which are won by the individual with the most willpower rather than the one with the greatest degree of truth on his side. So, conversations, yes...arguments, no! During conversation, questions are raised and answered or tabled. There are even times in conversations that call for two parties to respectfully disagree about an issue. Unlike in an argument, such disagreements are often a cause for exploration rather than explosion. Conversations entail a healthy respect for others. I have conversations with people with whom I have relationships. In fact, conversation is one of the most intimate ways we relate to other humans.

Presentations, on the other hand, are cold and lifeless. They demand that I stay on topic. If I'm presenting something to you, I'm not going to appreciate distractions or interruptions. Presentations don't lend themselves well to questions. Most of the time, I've only *memorized* the actual presentation itself, so if you try to ask me about a peripheral issue, I'm lost! Presentations are all about facts— facts that I must deliver to you; facts that you must accept; facts that we must agree on in the end or I will need to go through the presentation again with you until you *do* agree with me! Worst of all, presentations are impersonal. I've sat through lectures and sales pitches many times. Never once did I feel like I really connected with the person attempting to sway my thinking!

If you're married, I'm sure you already get what I'm talking about. I am a very logical person. That means that for me the best way to make a decision is to lay out all of the facts. I then consider the pros and cons of a decision along with the inherent risks, and BOOM, I know what to do. However, I learned very early on in my marriage that my wife Wendy is not like me. She doesn't want me to present a list of facts to her in an attempt to convince her of the most logical thing to do. She also doesn't want me to analyze all the issues or problems that she brings up so that I can offer the best logical answer. When she comes home lamenting a hard day at work or talking about a new frustration, she's not looking for me to diagnose her problem and present her with facts. No, she wants to *talk about things*. I would be happy with presentations, but she wants conversations. Sometimes this truth frustrates me because it means that making decisions requires a much longer process, and that I have to be *real*. You see, she doesn't want to feel like I'm simply a business partner. She wants to feel like we relate to one another and that we connect! So, over the years I've had to learn the art of relating to her through conversation.

The beautiful thing I've learned in all of this is that the greatest benefit of conversation is its relationality. Yes, I know that I just totally made up a word. Really talking to someone draws on the power of the relationship—the connecting that happens through it all. It opens people up to consider things that they never would consider otherwise. People may tune out my presentation, but there's something authentic, real, and personal that is birthed out of conversation. Perhaps the reason that we so often feel like we get nowhere with our gospel presentations is because they are just that… cold, dead, lifeless facts. People don't feel the passion, the joy, or the relationality of the gospel message unless we find a way to connect with them personally. This should not be surprising to us since the gospel itself is inherently relational! Jesus' dying on a cross for my sin is not a matter of fact; it's a matter of love!

I firmly believe that a majority of people grow to Jesus rather than have a Damascus Road experience like Paul. Just as I grew to love my wife, I became acquainted with Jesus through the life of someone else and grew to love Him and realize my need for Him. Most of us see Christ at work in others or have a growing feeling of a need for something that is missing until we discover that He is the answer. So, the point is that as we connect with people, we need to become comfortable with bringing up spiritual issues, having spiritual conversations, sharing our own faith stories when possible, and doing all of these within the context of relationship.

All of that having been said, let me propose a danger that each of us may run into when it comes to this approach. If we're not careful, we can elevate the importance of an individual relationship *above* the importance of a person's hearing about and having the opportunity to come to faith in Christ. Spiritual conversations won't just happen automatically. You have to be intentional about bringing up faith issues. Don't fall into the trap of spending so much time trying to cultivate a great relationship that you leave out the most important connecting point of all. I believe we are sometimes afraid of bringing up spiritual issues with people we care about because we're afraid those conversations may cause damage to the relationship. I would suggest that, as long as you focus on fostering the connection, it's very possible to talk about some of the most controversial things and see relationships strengthened rather than destroyed. There is, after all, an intimacy that comes with being transparent with others.

This truth leads to my being very clear about something, and I say this with as much love as possible. If your friends, family members, coworkers, neighbors, gym pals, and all others in your life do not have relationships with Christ then they are missing out on an abundant life here on earth, but more importantly, they are bound for an eternity separated from life, love, joy, happiness, and true peace! And if you and I are truly concerned about those we love…

if the relationships are really so important to us…wouldn't we want those relationships to continue into eternity? Wouldn't we want our friends and loved ones to have a relationship with the one individual in all of the universe with whom they were made to be in a relationship?

Imagine the disappointment that is going to take place at judgment when people realize that they will experience an eternity separated from God and that some of the very people who will experience God's joy and peace were folks with whom they had close friendships. Think of the ones you know who you're pretty sure haven't experienced saving faith. Do you think that they'll be happy with your silence as they stand in judgement? Do you think they'll really be glad you didn't take the chance of shaking up the relationship? Will they see your decision not to bring up spiritual issues as an act of love? I think not! This is precisely why I feel that you and I must do everything in our power to leverage every relationship we have for the glory of God, the growth of His kingdom, and the good of people who don't yet know Him.

I believe that there are at least 5 very real and compelling reasons that we must take every opportunity we can to build spiritual bridges within the context of our relationships. These 5 reasons should constantly remind us that every bond we have is an opportunity that's been afforded to us by God to connect someone to Him. Each is a Biblical reality that should encourage us as we obediently share our own faith stories or haunt us as we keep silent. These are 5 reasons that we must share! So, what are they? I'm glad you asked…here we go!

REASON 1: CHRIST COMMANDS IT

Have you ever thought about the importance of last words? Imagine that you're standing in the room as I lie there taking the last breaths at the end of my life. I'm surrounded by my wife, my children, their spouses, my grandchildren. I've lived a long life and am spending my last moments on this earth with those who mean the most to me and, hopefully, those who've learned the most from me in my time on earth. As the end draws near, I have time for just a few last words—just one or two things that I can say to encourage my wife and lift up my children. These are the words they'll remember moments after I'm gone. These are the words that they will talk about over the next weeks and months as they process my passing and deal with their grief. These are the words that they will recall years from now when my children say to their children, "I remember the last thing your grandfather said to me. It meant so much that I want to pass it on to you."

Now, imagine that as you stand there watching this unfold, I look at my wife and say, "Honey, you know I love you. Don't forget to feed the chickens and pay the bills on time." Or, I look at my oldest son and say, "Son, I know you're going to miss me, but remember what I always taught you: take out the trash every day and never leave dirty clothes lying on the floor." Would my choice of words surprise you? I'm sure they would because you and I both know that last words are some of the most important ones we will ever speak! These are the words that mark one's legacy and perhaps chart the course of life for those who are left behind. This fact is exactly why a father's final blessing was so important in Old Testament times. Last words matter. In fact, they matter so much that some folks are willing to live their lives and possibly even go to their deaths because of last words which were spoken to them by someone they love and admire.

So it is then that when Jesus, the most influential person to ever walk the earth, speaks His last words, those closest to Him, the ones who truly love Him, listen! Every single gospel writer in the New Testament records these important last words of Jesus. And, across the board, they all focus on and revolve around one central theme. No matter the perspective, the truth is the same: "Lead others to believe in Me!" Having just completed the work of making salvation possible, Jesus determines the legacy and work by which His followers will go on to be known: namely introducing others and leading others to saving faith in Him. Having made salvation available, He leaves it to His followers to make it accessible.

IIn Matthew 28:18-20, we read what is referred to in Christian circles as the Great Commission. In these most famous of last words, Jesus makes a couple of things clear to His disciples:

> "All authority has been given to Me in heaven and on
> earth. Go, therefore, and make disciples of all nations,
> baptizing them in the name of the Father and of the
> Son and of the Holy Spirit, teaching them to observe
> everything I have commanded you. And remember, I
> am with you always, to the end of the age."

First off, notice that Jesus addresses the issue of authority at the very beginning. He wants His listeners to know that He has every right to demand of them what He is about to ask. The command that He gives is not based on the request of an equal, but the right of an emperor! The same voice that spoke the universe into being now gives a parting command to His followers. And the same authority Jesus claimed before the disciples two thousand years ago rests securely in his hands today. He has the same power to command you and me.

Based on this authority, Jesus commands His disciples in all times and at all places to "go...and make disciples." In the original language, the word "go" is actually a participle that can be translated "as you are going" or even "as you conduct your life." It's much more about a continuation of action rather than the location of action. In other words, Jesus isn't nearly as concerned about where you go as He is about *how* you go. What He demands is that *as we go,* regardless of where that may be, you and I must be intentional about the task of making disciples who we will then teach to become reproducing disciple-makers themselves.

The author of the Gospel of Mark puts it this way: "Go into all the world and preach the gospel to the whole creation. Whoever believes and is baptized will be saved, but whoever does not believe will be condemned."[vi] Mark makes it clear that the focus of our going is the world. Until the entire world has had the opportunity to hear the gospel of Jesus, believers like you and me are to continue to go! Notice that our success in following Christ is only dependent on our going and our preaching (or sharing), not on whether people actually respond in faith. It's completely up to those with whom we share as to whether they will believe and act on what they hear. However, we are specifically breaking a key command of Christ when we choose not to take the gospel of Christ to those who haven't heard.

In the book of John, Jesus claims the following: "As the Father has sent Me, I also send you."[vii] Jesus specifically ties the task He gives His followers to do to the work that He Himself has been doing for His Father. I don't know if you've ever really thought about evangelism in this light, but when you and I actively share our faith with others, we are participating in a redemption plan that was orchestrated and put into motion by the Creator of the universe Himself. We are continuing His work. Obedience to His command to go involves us in something infinitely bigger than ourselves!

The Gospel of Luke is a detailed account of Jesus' life, ministry, and the redemption brought about through His sacrifice. The sequel to Luke's account of the story of Christ is the book of Acts. In this sequel to his gospel, Luke continues the story, revealing how earliest Christians put Jesus' command into action. Luke's recollection of the Great Commission is found in the first chapter of the book of Acts. Here, Jesus says, "You will receive power when the Holy Spirit has come upon you, and you will be My witnesses in Jerusalem, in all Judea and Samaria, and to the ends of the earth."[viii] I would like to point out a couple of things here.

First, notice that Jesus speaks of a future certainty when He states that His followers "will" be witnesses. Jesus does not presume that His true followers have any choice but to share what they know of Him. They can not keep the message to themselves. He doesn't present any conditions or exceptions here. He simply says that His true followers *will* be witnesses.

There are some who make much of Jesus' mention of specific locales here. It's been said by many that Jesus is making it clear that He wants His disciples to start where they are (Jerusalem) and work outwards towards the world as they share. I don't necessarily disagree with that teaching. In fact, I believe that there is truth in it. However, if you understand the Jewish culture of that time, you may realize that something else is going on here as well.

Jesus is not unveiling a strategic plan for the spread of the gospel as much as He is making a statement about the universal need for the gospel. The folks that Jesus was talking to were all Jews. In mentioning Jerusalem, He's making it clear that the gospel is for people who are like them. It's for their families, friends, co-workers, and neighbors; but the gospel wasn't just for them. It was also for their country-men, folks with whom they had no relationship, but with whom they had things in common. Furthermore, it was also for people with whom they had little in common and possibly even despised!

Jews hated the Samaritans and saw the rest of the world as pagan. I believe that Jesus is making it clear to His listeners that, though they may start with those *relationally* closest to them, He intended for them to take the gospel to everyone, even those whom they may consider to be their greatest enemies. In other words, start with what is familiar and continually move towards that which is unfamiliar. Of course, this would mean that they would be forced to find some way to forge relationships with these people! And get this…the first few chapters of the book of Acts demonstrate this very thing happening as Christians leave Jerusalem under the threat of persecution. Wherever they went, these believers established new relationships and Christian churches sprang to life.

Again, we see at the very heart of the gospel command an inherent relationality! If you and I claim to follow Jesus, then there is never a point at which we should feel let off the hook from sharing our faith. Furthermore, we must realize that Jesus expects us to intentionally deepen every relationship we have as we work to see friends, co-workers, strangers, and even enemies transformed into brothers and sisters in Christ. Why share our faith? We share because Jesus expects it and commands it!

REASON 2: HELL IS REAL

You know as well as I do that hell is not a popular topic in today's world, not even in our churches. That's partially because hell is such a bad place. However, another reason that so many people have an issue with hell is because they find it hard to reconcile the concept of such a horrible place with a completely loving and merciful God. Many say that there is no way a loving God would really send people to hell. Others believe that if there is a hell, it's only reserved for the worst monsters of humanity. These people feel that a relatively good person has no need to worry that he might end up in hell. While we will get to some of these concerns later in the book, one thing needs to be made clear right now: *hell is real!* This truth should be a driving factor for our work of evangelism even if there were no command given for us to share!

No truly informed reading of the New Testament could deny the reality of hell. While the goal of Scripture is to point us to the One who intends to rescue us for eternal life and joy, there is no doubt that Christ describes an antithesis for those who choose not to believe! The question is "What is hell really like?" Well, to find the answer to that question, let's see what Jesus has to say about the issue.

First of all, look at a parable that Jesus shares concerning two men.[ix] One of these was rich and apparently pretty selfish, living it up while on earth. The other, a beggar, was a righteous and God-fearing man. The first feasted in luxury with no regard to the needs of others while the latter sat starving at his gate. Both men died with Lazarus, the righteous man, ending up in paradise at "Abraham's side" and the rich man finding himself in "Hades."

In the story, Jesus makes it clear that "Hades," a term often used in the place of hell in the New Testament, is a place of torment, flames, and extreme agony. Though we can't confidently say whether or not Lazarus could see into hell, it's abundantly obvious that those in hell could see into paradise. Think about how this must exacerbate their torturous condition. Evidently, not only do those in hell experience eternal torment, but they are constantly reminded that they could have had something infinitely better had they but believed. Not only will they experience the physical pain that abides in such a place, but they will also feel the emotional agony that goes along with seeing those they have loved or shared relationships with delighting in the joys of heaven without them. Abraham goes on to explain that there is a great "chasm" between the two places so that no one may cross. In other words, hell is permanent. There is no exit once someone enters.

In another teaching, Jesus addresses the seriousness of temptation and sin saying, "If your hand causes your downfall, cut if off. It is better for you to enter life maimed than to have two hands and go to hell - the unquenchable fire, where their worm does not die, and the fire is not quenched."ˣ Obviously, Jesus is not advocating self-mutilation here. Rather, He is taking a very hard stance on sin and temptation. In other words, if there is anything in our lives that causes our downfall, we must remove it at all costs. Notice what He has to say about hell. First He says the fire is unquenchable. I've often heard it said that to die by burning is one of the most painful ways to go. Can you imagine, even for a moment, burning for all of eternity in an unquenchable fire, realizing one thousand years into it that you are no closer to the end than when you began? Think about the psychological torture this would inflict. Remarkably, according to Jesus, the flame isn't all we have to endure. There are also the worms. I'm not sure what these worms are up to, but you can rest assured it's not good or Jesus wouldn't have mentioned them. Could these be maggots or some other kind of flesh-eating parasite? It's not made clear, but, regardless, we're told that they never die either!

In Matthew 8:11-12, Jesus gives more details about hell. Here, He indicates that hell is also a place of utter darkness. I have heard people say before that they are alright with going to hell because they know they will have friends there. In their minds, hell is going to be an eternal party filled with all types of carousing. Jesus, on the other hand, says that hell will be a place of "weeping and gnashing of teeth." I would challenge you to think back to the story of the rich man for a moment. Was there any mention of the friends that he had partied with while on earth? No! I believe that is because hell is a place of utter darkness. And that darkness exponentially intensifies the loneliness of the place. You see, it's not just a relationship with God that is severed by hell, it's the possibility of any relationship, period!

There will be no parties in hell! There will be no enjoyment in hell! Why? Because there can be no *joy* in hell! Anything that we find enjoyable in this world will be noticeably absent in hell. What people don't realize is that our ability to enjoy anything is a gift from God. James 1:17 tells us that "every generous act and every perfect gift is from above, coming down from the Father of lights." Therefore, if there is anything in this world that is pleasurable—if there is even an ability to enjoy—that thing will not be in hell. In hell there is only misery. It is a place of eternal punishment for God's enemies, not a place where exists even the remotest possibility of comfort or peace. Hell is real...and it's really bad!!!

REASON 3: PEOPLE ARE REALLY GOING TO HELL

The idea that people will go to hell is, perhaps, one of the hardest concepts for some to grasp. There is a basic premise in our society that most people are good folks at the core of their being. I would agree, to a point, that many people want to do what they think is right and genuinely do care about others. I believe that these characteristics are a remnant of the original image of God placed within man. However, make no mistake, there really is no such thing as a good person!

I have had the pleasure throughout the years of being around children and teenagers quite a bit. My undergraduate degree is in elementary education. I actually taught seventh and eighth grade math for a few years in public school. I spent many hours in kindergarten and second grade classrooms during college years. I've worked as a children's minister, and I have children of my own. One thing I've had confirmed for me over the years, as I've watched interactions between children, is that they are all, indeed, born with a sin nature. I challenge you to watch some toddlers on the playground for a while, and I know you'll agree! No one has to teach children to be selfish or bossy or mean; it just comes naturally. While we learn to control ourselves a bit more as we grow into adulthood, the truth remains that in any given situation, you and I have an equal chance of choosing to do wrong as we do of choosing what's right. This fact is just part of who we are!

The argument has been made over and over again that God can't be a loving God if He sends good people to such a horrible place as hell. I would wholeheartedly agree with this statement. If God sends *good* people to hell, then He most definitely is not a good and loving God! The problem is that we have a distorted view of the inherent goodness of humanity. Truthfully, this "good person" that so many people talk about doesn't exist! There are no good people in the world. We are all broken, filthy, unregenerate products of a fallen race. Whether we like or not...whether we admit it or not... we are all rotten to the core!

You might ask, "If we're all so rotten, then how do people do good things?" Well, people do good things in spite of their true nature, not because of it. The good they do is specifically attributable to God. Scripture puts it this way: "There is no one righteous, not even one; there is no one who understands, there is no one who seeks God. All have turned away; together they have become useless; there is no one who does good; there is not even one."[xi] So there is not even one good, righteous person among us. We are all tainted by sin. This means that there is no good person for God to allow into heaven based on his own merit. That person just doesn't exist! There are many more passages in the Bible that back up this truth. Though we may do some good things every now and then, people are inherently sinful beings! While many struggle with the concept of a loving God sending people to hell, we must ask ourselves how God could possibly be good and loving if He doesn't send people to hell who actually deserve it. If He allows evil into a perfectly sinless place, then He is the worst kind of fiend! You see, hell exists precisely because God is so good: He's fair, and that means that evil must be punished! The plain truth is that hell is real and people really deserve to go there!

Let's be clear about something here—though mankind deserves it, it's not God's desire for people to go to hell! In fact, the apostle Peter tells us that the Lord "is patient with you, not wanting any to perish, but all to come to repentance."[xii] In fact, God is so passionate about people's missing hell and having heaven that He took matters into His own hands and made a way through the sacrifice of His own Son. Christ willingly endured God's wrath against sin in our place. For those of us who place our faith in Him, Christ's holiness is substituted for our innate sinfulness. Those who were formally evil have been made good through His sacrifice. That's the beautiful message of the gospel.

The story goes deeper from there. You might wonder why people still go to hell even after the cross. People go to hell precisely because God loves them. God offers a free gift of redemption and forgiveness, but He does so on His terms. In order to be saved, one must turn from his selfish and sinful lifestyle and follow Christ. Not everyone is willing to do this. In fact, the only way some people would end up in heaven is against their own will. God, being the perfect gentleman, will not force Himself on anyone. You can choose to accept the gift He offers through His Son, or you can choose to reject it. He will not force salvation on you! To force those who are completely free and capable of making their own decisions to violate their standards and live their lives according to your own ideals is to disrespect their basic rights as human beings...in essence, you make them slaves. Obviously, to do such a thing would not be considered loving. What this means is that the default state in which every single person in this world exists is condemnation. You and I, our neighbors, co-workers, friends, and even those living in the deepest and darkest parts of the jungles of South America are all born into the world condemned. Our only chance for salvation is found in Jesus who is "the way, the truth, and the life. No one comes to the Father except through [Him]."xiii

Now, while you and I may know and believe this, there are countless millions who don't. In fact, the prevalent religious viewpoint among most people is that there is some way to earn one's way into heaven. Many people see themselves as good people and believe that they will be allowed into an eternal paradise based on their own merit or that as long as all of their good outweighs their bad, God will choose to look the other way and allow them into heaven. Some believe that there is inherent truth in all religions, and thus they all lead to a better place. There will be countless numbers of people who will be horribly disappointed as they stand in judgment, however, to find that there is no possibility of their ever being good enough to earn heaven on their own.

There is one passage in the Bible that gives us a very clear picture of what this scene is going to look like. In His Sermon on the Mount, Jesus explains that there are two ways to follow in this world. One is difficult, narrow, and few find it. This way, of course, leads to salvation. The other is wide, easy, and is followed by many, but ultimately leads to destruction. He goes on to talk about false prophets who seem to have a righteousness of their own, but don't produce fruit as a result of His indwelling Spirit. Outwardly, these people appear to be on the correct path, but inwardly they are not! These are people of whom the rest of the world would speak little evil. They are looked up to by many and seen as spiritually elite because they seem to be such *good* people. Listen, however, to Jesus' words concerning judgment for these folks:

> "Not everyone who says to Me, 'Lord, Lord!' will enter
> the kingdom of heaven, but only the one who does
> the will of My Father in heaven. On that day many
> will say to Me, 'Lord, Lord, didn't we prophesy in

> Your name, drive out demons in Your name, and do
> many miracles in Your name?' Then I will announce
> to them, 'I never knew you! Depart from Me, you
> lawbreakers!'"xiv

This is, in my opinion, one of the scariest passages in all of Scripture. Notice that these people thought they were doing all the right things in order to earn favor with God. They truly believed that they were good people, deserving of heaven. It never crossed their minds until it was too late that all of their actions would have no bearing on their eternal state. Note the way they tried to throw all of their good deeds at the feet of Jesus as an appeal that they were deserving of eternal life. Jesus' response? He sent them away because they had no relationship with Him! What we learn from this passage is that, just as in many other areas of life, it's not what you do or who you are that determines your future. It's, rather, Who you know! Only those who know Jesus and, more importantly, who are *known* by Jesus will inherit eternal life.

This stark reality should drive us to spend every waking moment doing all we can to educate and convince those around us that their good deeds are not enough to guarantee them an eternity with God. Mankind doesn't need to do more to be right with God; they need Jesus in order to be right with God. If you have Jesus, you have life; however, those without Jesus *already* stand condemned. The truth? Hell is real…and it's really bad! And because people—regardless of how good they think they are—stand condemned apart from Jesus, they will really go there!

REASON 4: GOD HAS MADE A WAY!

Imagine with me for a moment how hopeless would be our case had God decided to leave us in our rebellion. The reality of hell would be unavoidable. The fact that people would go there would eternally stand as both incomprehensible and unbearable. If only those two facts were true, what a hopeless lot we would be. Praise God, however, that He chose to intervene! That God has provided a way of escape from such a destructive end should not only blow our minds but should also embolden us to share this message of rescue with everyone we know!

Imagine that you were to come out of your favorite store to see a friend sitting inside his car in the parking lot. As you wave at him, you notice that there is something odd about the scene before you. Inspecting further, you realize that there are flames coming from beneath the car. Though unseen by your friend, you know that if you do not get him out of the car he will certainly die. Now imagine that as you yell and wave frantically for your friend to get out of the car, he ignores you. Would you stop? Absolutely not! I'm sure this would only strengthen your resolve to get him out. What if he refuses to open the door once you get to the car? What if he yells out to you that he smells no smoke and that he thinks you are just being an alarmist or unrealistic or that you are crazy? Would you then walk away? Not if you're a good friend! I'm sure that you would do all within your power to get him out of that vehicle, even if it meant breaking the window and dragging him out! Why? Because you know something he doesn't. You realize he is headed towards torment and suffering, but more importantly, you know there's a way out! Whether he believes you or whether your intervention could potentially damage the relationship is of no issue. You would act simply because you know of a way to prevent his destruction!

I hope you can see the spiritual significance of this illustration. All of us have people in our lives with whom we have relationships whose lives are headed for destruction. Hell is real…it's really bad…and, people are really going there! However, God has made a way out! How can we not share this? How can we not shout it from the roof tops? How can we not leverage every moment of communication to introduce this wonderful news to those we care about and love? The only answer I can come up with is that, perhaps, we don't fully comprehend the enormity of this ourselves!

We've talked about John 14:6, where Jesus made the following claim: "I am the way, the truth, and the life. No one comes to the Father except through Me." We often focus on the exclusivity of this statement and the fact that Jesus claims to be the only way. Let me propose we consider another aspect of this for a moment. Have you ever stopped to consider just how amazing it is that God would provide *a way* in the first place? He's certainly not obligated to do so! He doesn't owe us anything. In fact, it's just the opposite. He doesn't need anything from us. We have no way of repaying Him. The truth is that you and I have rebelled against God in our sin! We are His enemies! Yet, HE MADE A WAY!!! If this doesn't excite you, you may need to check your pulse!

Paul in his letter to the Romans makes the beauty of this clear when he says that "God proves His own love for us in that while we were still sinners, Christ died for us!"[xv] God doesn't demand that we get cleaned up before He will consider taking us in. He doesn't require that we demonstrate our loyalty to Him or His cause before He is willing to prove loyal to us. There are no religious hoops we must jump through in order to come to Him. God doesn't insist on only helping those who are willing to help themselves. God doesn't promise to love you if you will but love Him. No, before you or I had any inkling of repentance or desire to act on faith, God took it upon Himself to make a way. While we were still sinners—enemies—God demonstrated His love by sending His only Son to make a way for us to come back!

Go all the way back to the fall of mankind in the Garden of Eden.[xvi] Eve, followed closely by Adam, chose to give up a rich relationship

34

with God in an act of rebellion, a vain attempt at autonomy and self-reliance. In doing so, they set themselves up, not just against God, but in the place of God. In their hearts and lives, God was dethroned. This is more than disloyalty…this is anarchy…treason! And so man has reigned upon his throne of sinful passion and indulgence ever since, supplanting the righteous will of God with His own will, all the while suffering the consequences of his betrayal. Yet God, in His great love, had a plan from the beginning to set everything right again. He would make a way for those who had rebelled against Him to be ransomed! He would create an opportunity for those who would take His throne by force to be brought into His family and to be made joint-heirs with Christ. Oh, the insanity of His love! And we would keep this great message to ourselves?!

This wonderful story climaxes, of course, in the redemptive act of the cross. One of the most well-known passages in the Bible tells us clearly that "God loved the world in this way: He gave His One and Only Son, so that everyone who believes in Him will not perish but have eternal life. For God did not send His Son into the world that He might condemn the world, but that the world might be saved through Him. Anyone who believes in Him is not condemned, but anyone who does not believe is already condemned."xvii In His atoning death and resurrection, Jesus has become the way for a lost world to find salvation. I've heard it said before that religion is man reaching to God, but the cross is God reaching to man. He has made a way!

What kind of person knows that certain doom is awaiting those they love, but refuses to offer them a way out? My friends, there is a command to share our faith, and the One who gives the command has every right to do so. There is imminent destruction awaiting those who don't receive the gift. Hell is real…it's really bad…and people will really go there! Ah, but most amazing is the reality that the God of the universe took the initiative, when you and I could not, to make a way! He has made a way, and we must not keep that to ourselves!

REASON 5: SOME WILL BELIEVE

Over the years, I have had many opportunities to have spiritual conversations with people. Some of these conversations have led to outcomes resulting in new relationships with Christ while others have not. I have forgotten the circumstances surrounding most of these, but there are a couple which stand out vividly in my mind.

Not long after I started in ministry, the church in which I was serving decided to canvass a neighborhood, going door to door in an attempt to share the gospel. I will confess that this felt awkward to me as I wondered how people would respond to a complete stranger's showing up at their door to share something so intimate. I guess you could say that I felt like an encyclopedia or vacuum salesman to a degree. We were three houses into our assigned street when a door was opened by a man who was obviously startled to see a group of smiling Christians. As I began talking to him about his church affiliation and asking if I could share what I believed, he quickly cut me off. "Young man, I don't have any need for your church or your God! You Christians are weak-minded people. Leave my home and never come back!" As you can imagine, I was quite taken aback by this response. Trying to ensure him of his need for Christ only made things worse; so I finally admitted defeat, said I'd pray for him, and reluctantly led my group back outside. To say the confrontation affected our attitude the rest of the night—and even for weeks to come—is an understatement! The truth is that for years after that experience, every time I had the opportunity to share with someone, I remembered that guy!

During seminary I was a part-time youth pastor at a small church in Cleburne, Texas. My years there were some of the most formative of my life. I was surrounded by youth workers who loved the Lord and worked alongside me in constantly challenging our young people to take every opportunity they had to make their faith known to their friends. Though I was struggling to really figure out the proper approach to evangelism, it was here that I enjoyed some very rich relationships that resulted in people's coming to the Lord. I specifically remember one of my youth whom we will call Chip. Chip was a golfer, and boy was he great at the game! Every week or so, I would try to get together with Chip and a couple of other guys to play a round of golf. Some of the things that happened on that Cleburne golf course were hilarious. We found out that golf carts can be used as amphibious vehicles. We learned how to drift in a golf cart. We found out that a golf cart against the door of a portable toilet is nearly impossible to budge. And, being the worst player in the group, I got a great education in golf. Perhaps the most memorable thing, though, happened on a warm day in between the ninth and tenth holes at the little burger joint on the course. It was on that day that the conversation turned to spiritual matters, and Chip realized that he had never personally made Jesus his Lord and Savior. Right there, between holes nine and ten, he gave his heart and life to Christ! Needless to say, my game on the back nine was much greater that day than it had been on the front! Of all the fun times I had with those guys, that day stands head and shoulders above the rest!

Why do I share these stories with you? To make one point: obviously, not everyone with whom you share your faith story will make a decision to follow Christ, but if you are faithful, you can rest assured that some will! What if I had let my bad experience with evangelism paralyze me to the point that I never shared my faith again? What if I had not intentionally tried to turn things in a spiritual direction on that summer day with Chip? I will not falsely presume, nor will

I lead you to do so, that everyone with whom you share your faith will listen, believe, and call on the name of Jesus. I will promise you, however, that if you are faithful in leveraging every relationship you have for the glory of God and good of others, some will respond in faith! Some of those people you care so much about *will be saved!!!*

In his opening description of the work of Jesus, John tells us the following about Christ and His work:

> "But to all who did receive Him, He gave them the
> right to be children of God, to those who believe in
> His name, who were born, not of blood, or of the will
> of the flesh, or of the will of man, but of God."[xviii]

Everyone who will faithfully receive the gift of salvation will be made a child of God. This is an amazing promise! Notice also that John says these are not children "born of blood, or the will of the flesh, or of the will of man." In other words, there is no chance behavior or human action preceding this rebirth. Instead, it is an adoptive act that is dependent upon the will of the Father. The Father desires the salvation of mankind, and we have His promise that anyone who responds will be brought into the family. Some will believe… and be saved!

We read this promise again in Romans 10:13 where Paul claims that "everyone who calls on the name of the Lord will be saved." Did you catch that? Everyone! God will not desert the one who calls out to Him in faith! As we share our faith stories, some will come under conviction of their need for a Savior. Some will hear. Some will listen. Some will believe and will call upon the name of the Lord. Some will be saved!

I fully believe that we tend to live life according to negatives. What I mean by this is that most of us go through life in a constant effort to continually play it safe, enhancing positives and eliminating negatives. We want to avoid confrontation, avoid discomfort, avoid pain, and avoid making waves. We play it safe at our jobs. We play it safe with our sports. We play it safe in our families. We play it safe in our relationships. Instead of willfully risking our lives on a daily basis, we seek to mitigate risk. This tendency, I believe, is precisely the reason some of us refuse to share our faith. There is a risk involved. Sharing my faith story with a coworker carries an inherent risk. Crossing that line with a friend could potentially drive her away. Bringing up faith issues with family members may make life more difficult. What this all boils down to is that we are often silent about Jesus and others' need for Him because the risk of rejection is more abhorrent to us than the reality of their destruction.

I will honestly tell you that there are inherent risks that go along with sharing the gospel. I would also encourage you by reminding you that the risks are more than worth it because, though some may reject Christ, others with whom you share will believe! Some will be saved!

CONCLUSION

I hope you see the thread that runs through all 5 of these reasons to share. That thread is relationship! Our relationship with Christ is a catalyst to our sharing Christ in every other relationship. Our love for others fuels our desire to see them come into relationship with Him. The hope that some will join in a joyous relationship with Jesus keeps us going even when we experience rejection after rejection. Evangelism is, indeed, inherently relational. If you have a relationship with Christ, it is incumbent upon you to extend that relationship and its impact to every other relationship you have. Instead of exalting our relationships over people's need to hear about Christ, we should leverage every relationship to the maximum degree for God's glory, the growth of His kingdom, and the good of all people.

Sharing the gospel is, after all, what we have been left on this earth to do. Christ's authority in giving His Great Commission is without question. His desire for all people everywhere to hear the message of hope is beyond compare. He commands us to join Him in the work He began. This is a serious endeavor as the stakes are eternal. Destruction awaits those who die without Christ because the default state of every human being is condemnation. The reality of hell is intolerable, and the fact that people will actually go there should instill an unstoppable drive within believers to introduce sinners to the only way of salvation. God has made this way possible! And we have the calm assurance that, though some may reject the message of hope found in Christ, if we will but leverage our relationships for the spread of the gospel, some will believe and be saved!

These are the reasons we must take the opportunities afforded us daily in our relationships to have spiritual conversations. These reasons are why we must be authentic. These reasons are why we must allow God to use us and work through us. These reasons require intentionality in our relationships rather than aimlessness. These reasons inform us that every relationship we have is a tool for a universal and eternal purpose. These are the reasons we must share!

5

Prayers to Pray

Not too long ago, a church staff I was a part of felt the need to lead our church into deeper waters in the area of prayer. We knew that we had to set the example in this area by creating opportunities for corporate prayer to happen more naturally and more often. We began by reorganizing our church schedule to create more space for prayer during the week and by evaluating our current prayer emphases in light of Scripture. Our goal was to lead the church to become intentional in prayer and to see our church members united by praying for specific areas of personal, corporate, and global need. We specifically challenged our members to pray for the spread of the gospel and the growth of God's kingdom.

I vividly remember leading one of the first prayer services. As I talked about the importance of prayer for evangelism and our desperate need for Christ to go before us in this area, the Holy Spirit clearly laid on my heart the truth that God is always faithful to work when His people are united in prayer. A mighty working of God is always preceded by a movement of prayer among His people. "Prayer precedes power" became one of the hooks upon which we hung our corporate prayer lives. Did you know that every great revival in history began with a group of people who were praying for God to step in and make Himself known? As the weeks went by, we kept coming back to this phrase as a reminder that one of the most amazing and effective things that we can do as believers is pray for God to intervene in our world.

It's true, you know: Prayer really does precede power! An important aspect that is foundational in our understanding of God is the notion that God, being the perfect gentleman, will not force Himself into any situation to which He's not invited. This truth is precisely the reason that many religious leaders believe that God is ready and willing to do so much more than His people could ever ask or dream if they would just put Him to the test. The truth is that prayer is one of the most under-utilized tools at the Christian's disposal.

Get this: according to a study carried out at San Francisco General Medical Center, there is a direct and measurable correlation between prayer and the well-being of those for whom people pray. As part of the study, patients were randomly divided into placebo and test groups. Christians prayed for the folks in the test group while those in the placebo group were not prayed for. It should come as no surprise that, though there were no statistical differences between the two groups *before* the study, the group that was prayed for demonstrated markedly better health after the study began. The patients that were prayed for suffered fewer medical problems than those who weren't![xix] Surprising? I should say not! As people of faith, you and I understand that prayer precedes power. When God's people pray, God acts!

If you're a believer, I'm sure I'm preaching to the choir. Indeed, almost all followers of Christ would be quick to acknowledge the importance of prayer in the life of the Christian. "Prayer meeting," as it's come to be called in many churches, is a regularly attended event at which God's people spend a great deal of time praying for those who are sick, dying, or hurting in some way. These individuals are prayed for by name as believers commit themselves to interceding for them until healing or relief is realized. I know from experience that believers are quick to pray for the physical and emotional needs surrounding them, but I would challenge all believers with one question. What if we spent as much time praying for the spiritual sicknesses and needs surrounding us as we do for physical needs? What if you and I had prayer lists filled with the names of folks whom we knew had no relationship with Christ? Furthermore, what if we committed ourselves to praying for these people on a daily basis until they came to a saving knowledge of Jesus? Would that make a difference?

I believe that we would see a few outcomes from this endeavor. First of all, I believe we'd be more cognizant of those around us with spiritual needs. When we start recognizing the spiritual ailments around us, it becomes clear rather quickly that many of the physical and emotional needs we pray for on a regular basis are rooted in spiritual issues! We pray for broken families, but often lose sight of the fact that even one person that doesn't know Christ can completely throw the balance off in a home. We pray for someone to experience healing from cancer or some other type of disease, but often overlook the cancer of the soul that leads to spiritual death. These are the connections we begin to make when we regularly pray for lostness. Secondly, I believe that constant prayer for those who don't know Jesus would create a passionate desire within us to see those people saved. Think about it…if you pray on a daily basis for something to happen, doesn't the desire for that thing increase with time? Don't you become more and more desperate to see it come about? This fact brings me to the third outcome I think we'd see. We would seek ways to better position ourselves to become partners in the answering of these prayers. When we become desperate for something to happen, we naturally start looking for ways to bring about the desires of our hearts.

These three things point to one incredible truth about a vibrant prayer life. Real prayer is not nearly as much about changing God's heart as it is about changing our own! As we grow closer to God in prayer, our hearts begin to beat for the things for which His heart beats. We begin to see as He sees and desire what He desires. In other words, as we pray for spiritual problems, God begins to show us the role we play in the answer. This is especially true when it is an issue for which God is passionately desperate as well.

Trust me, there is no one who desires the salvation of your lost friends and family more than God! In fact, He did all the work to make salvation possible! When you and I make regular prayer for the lost a part of our conversation with God, His response is to show us how and where we can be involved in His pursuit for their souls. It is with this realization in mind that I suggest to you 5 things that you and I can pray on a daily basis for the lost around us. These are prayers that can be prayed in general for all lost people or can be prayed specifically for those you know. They are not magic formulas meant to rub some cosmic lamp, thus producing a genie-like response from God. He already desires the things you'll be praying for; however, God, being the perfect gentleman, will not often force Himself into a situation to which He has not been invited! By praying for your lost family and friends, you are inviting God to step in and you are partnering with Him in the task! In fact, what you may find in the end is that you are the very answer to the prayers you have been praying for the whole time! After all, prayer precedes power!

PRAYER 1: FOR GOD TO DRAW

I remember clearly the first time I met my wife. We were at a ninth grade science fair. I was doing an experiment on the aerodynamics of an airplane wing. Wendy was a few tables down presenting a project on a genetic trait in her family. We had mutual friends, but somehow we had never met before that day. I was talking with one of our friends when she joined our group. Honestly, at that moment I felt nothing. No chemistry, no fireworks, no "Wow, I gotta marry this girl!" I'm told that it was just the opposite for her. She fell in love with me right there in that moment. Just so you know that I'm not just bragging, let me assure you that she has backed this story up on numerous occasions...in fact, she's the one who shared it with me.

This first encounter marked the beginning of an up and down friendship that went on for about two and a half years before an underlying attraction to Wendy became apparent to me. As I look back over those years, one thing is crystal clear: though I wasn't initially interested in Wendy, she was very interested in me. She looked for opportunities to be around me. She found excuses for conversations. She even looked out for me in some pretty amazing ways—ways which I had no clue of at the time. I guess you could say she was "chasing" me. And here's what I discovered: the more she chased, and the more I got to know her, the more I was drawn to her. I'm being completely honest when I say that if it hadn't been for her, there's a very good chance that I would have never even asked her out on our first date. Wendy made it clear that she was available, but I had to be the one to invite her to join me in a relationship. Looking back, I know that had that first date not occurred, I would have missed the greatest thing next to Jesus that could possibly have happened to me in this life! You see, Wendy was there constantly drawing me in. All I had to do was accept her!

Now, here's where this whole story becomes good. Though I was drawn to her, I was completely clueless about how to begin a relationship with her. I guess you could say that I'm stupid in the ways of love! That's where Wendy stepped in again. As the story goes, she and some of her friends planned a party just to get the two of us together. Of course, I had no idea that the whole purpose of the event was to give me one last opportunity to begin a relationship with Wendy! Everything that went into the night was orchestrated in such a way that she and I ultimately found ourselves sitting alone talking. In that moment, she revealed to me how much she cared about me, and the light finally went on in my mind that I didn't just like this girl…I thought I might even love her! The next day, I called her and asked her out on our first date and life has never been the same! Oh, how sadly different my life would be today if Wendy had not chased me and drawn me in!

Now, you don't have to be a rocket scientist to notice some amazing correlations between my love story and the way that God works with each of us. God is madly in love with us! He desires a relationship with us. He's interested in us. He cares for us. He looks out for us. He chases us! He calls on the help of others whom He loves to assist in drawing us to Himself. These "friends" of God work alongside Him to create opportunities where we can be introduced to God, invited to know Him, and inspired to accept the relationship He so willingly offers. Do not miss an important truth, however; regardless of who is involved, God is most definitely the one who initiates each relationship!

In the sixth chapter of the Gospel of John, Jesus is seen having a conversation with a group of people who had been following Him around mainly because of the many miracles He had been performing. These folks weren't necessarily interested in Jesus in a spiritual way; rather, they were hoping for a few handouts. During His discourse, Jesus mentions that He will never reject anyone that the Father gives Him. This should be a great word of comfort to those of us who have come to Jesus, as it reveals the "eternality" of God's love and faithfulness towards us. As Jesus converses with some in the crowd, it is apparent that many do not believe in the legitimacy of His message. It is in response to these people that Jesus makes a remarkable statement: "'Stop complaining among yourselves. No one can come to Me unless the Father who sent me draws him.'"[xx]

Jesus is very clear in stating that anyone who responds to Him in saving faith does so precisely because the Father has initiated the relationship and drawn him. Now, at this point we could digress into a lengthy discussion about free will versus election, but that is most definitely a topic for another time and another book. Rather than arguing the finer points of reform theology or Armenian viewpoints, let's focus on what Jesus literally said. Jesus specifically and very pointedly said that the only people who come to Christ are those who have been drawn to Him by the Father. Whether you believe that God draws *all* people to Christ or whether you believe that He only draws the *elect* is really of no consequence here. The focus of the passage is God's drawing, not how He draws! So lets be clear: according to Jesus, no one comes to Him unless so drawn by the Father.

Just a little further in this same discourse, we see Jesus say the same thing in a different way as He speaks directly to His disciples. He reveals to them that He knows that some of them don't really believe in Him. They have their minds and hearts set on a political messiah and are missing the spiritual reality of what is before them. To these, Jesus says, "'There are some among you who don't believe....This is why I told you that no one can come to Me unless it is granted to him by the Father.'"[xxi] Again, Jesus makes it clear that God is the initiator every time someone places their faith in Jesus as Savior and Lord.

The knowledge and understanding of this truth, regardless of our opinions on the topic of predestination, should drive us to our knees in desperate prayer for our loved ones. Their only hope for salvation is for God to draw them! In fact, it is quite possible for them to live their lives in complete ignorance of His love, entering an eternity separated from Him precisely because they never felt the urgency of His invitation. We must passionately and pointedly pray that God will do everything in His power to draw the lost to Himself! We must pray that His love, care, and concern for them will be made known and understood. And we must pray that God would even use us as the instruments of His drawing! As God's "friends," you and I have the amazing opportunity to work alongside Him to create opportunities for people we know and love to be introduced to Him and the knowledge of what He's done for them.

Imagine how the lives of countless millions might be changed if believers would begin praying specifically every day for individuals to be drawn to God by whatever means possible. Imagine how the lives of your friends and family might be changed for eternity if you would be willing to commit yourself to continuously and constantly praying that the God of the universe would draw them to Himself and that He would use you as He does that. Just imagine…

PRAYER 2: FOR CHRISTIANS TO SHARE

As Jesus traveled through the country-side preaching, healing, and performing other signs and wonders, He picked up quite a following. To be sure, some of these were along for the show, hoping to see something bigger today than they saw the day before. There was great entertainment value in many of the things Jesus did. However, there were also those who were legitimately interested in what this carpenter turned Messiah had to say. They understood the truth of His words. They were drawn to His authenticity and His loving spirit. He spoke with an authority they had never heard before.

On one occasion, perhaps in the momentary pause of His everyday busy-ness, Jesus looked out over the crowds and felt a deep sense of empathy and compassion for them. Any study of Jesus' life would reveal that He had many such moments during His ministry. It was, however, at this particular point that Jesus made one of the most profound statements concerning our responsibility to pray for the lost and hurting. Understanding the heavy burden of sin these people carried and knowing the hopeless waywardness of their lives, He turned to His disciples and gave a command. "The harvest is abundant, but the workers are few. Therefore, pray to the Lord of the harvest to send out workers into His harvest."[xxii]

To what is Jesus referring when He mentions the harvest? Since no other mention of farming or fields is made, it would be unwise to assume that His statement is meant to be agricultural in nature. It is, instead, a metaphor for some deep spiritual truth. We know from immediate context that He's been looking out over the crowd. Therefore, the harvest must refer to the lost and burdened people who have been following Him. These are people who are seeking something greater than themselves. They are, though perhaps ignorant of the very fact, desperate for hope and meaning. Some are there specifically because they have been drawn by the Father and have begun to exhibit true faith in Jesus. Within this great crowd, there exists a harvest of souls!

Notice that Jesus says this harvest is abundant, but the workers are few. In other words, there are countless souls before them that are meant to be part of His harvest, yet there are few laborers doing the work of gathering. Jesus makes a very pointed statement when He claims that "the workers are few." He either speaks of disproportion or disobedience. Either He is saying that there are not enough laborers to gather the great harvest or that there are plenty of laborers, but they are not faithful to fulfill the obligation of their work. Regardless of the meaning, the truth stands that for those who would be faithful and obedient to gather, there is plenty of work to be had! This truth is just as applicable today as it was at the moment Jesus stated it. Right now, there is an innumerable quantity of people who have been drawn by the Father to know and accept the Son. Yet, there is great need of faithful and obedient workers to gather and bring these folks into the family of God.

I have to be honest with you. There is a gravity to this situation that haunts me as it should haunt you as well! Don't miss the fact that Jesus is insinuating there are a great number of people in this world who *would* choose Christ if they had the opportunity, but that they will not have that opportunity if His workers don't get about the task they've been given to do! Take a moment to contemplate the heaviness of this revelation. There are people who will be born, live their lives, die, and enter a devil's hell not because God isn't drawing them, but rather because Christians aren't being obedient in reaching them. God is doing the work of drawing people to Himself. The question is "Who is gathering the harvest?"

So Jesus, looking to His disciples, tells them what to do in order to remedy the situation. Pray, He commands, that God will send out workers. A little over two thousand years later, this command is just as poignant. You and I are to make constant requests that God will put a conviction in the hearts and minds of believers everywhere to share their faith with those around them. Quite honestly, if God's people were to regularly pray for God to draw lost people and for Christians to share their faith with lost people, the result would be a harvest of souls unlike anything we've seen since the days of the early church!

Now, let's be honest with each other about something. Too often, the reason we don't pray for God to send believers to reach the lost is because we are deathly afraid that the ones He might choose to send would be us or our children! In the past, I've had parents become upset with me for pushing teenagers to heavy involvement in evangelism because they were deathly afraid that their child might suddenly sense a call to missions and run off to the deepest, darkest parts of Africa. This attitude amazes me! As a parent of three children, I can think of no greater honor than for my children to become so passionately in love with Christ and His mission that they would be willing to forsake their hopes, dreams, and possibly even their lives to reach a world lost in sin and darkness. There is no greater calling! Is such a sacrifice painful? Yes! Is such a sacrifice worth it? Absolutely!

Get this, Christian: you and I have been commanded to share the gospel with those around us. There is no getting out of this command! Just as powerfully, we've been commanded to pray that God would send even more believers into the world to join in the task! Before He ever gave the command to go, Jesus instructed his followers to pray that there would be workers available to go! We not only have a Great Commission, but we have been called to make a Great Commitment to pray for believers to be about the task given them of sharing the faith.

Does the degree of lostness surrounding you drive you to your knees in prayer? Does the fact that Jesus has commanded you to pray for Christians to share create an obligation to do so within your heart? Would you be willing every day to pray that God would create a passionate desire in His children to share their faith with those around them? Would you give yourself to the constant request that God would send someone, *anyone*, to share the gospel message with your lost friends and family? Imagine how powerful it would prove if believers began praying regularly that God would send someone specifically to people they know of who need Jesus. Would you be willing to pray for exactly such a thing to happen? Furthermore, would you consider the possibility that, perhaps, you are the answer to that very prayer?

PRAYER 3: FOR DOORS TO OPEN

After receiving my undergraduate degree in education, I spent three years teaching middle school math before going to seminary. During those years, God taught me a few important things that I've been able to carry over into ministry. I learned that communicating for change was much more important than just communicating. I learned a deep appreciation and affection for young people. I developed a great love and passion for teaching, looking forward to seeing eyes light up with understanding as a new concept was grasped for the first time. This passion still burns within me. In fact, I tell people all the time that I'm just as much a teacher as I ever was. The only thing that has changed is my subject matter.

Perhaps the greatest thing I learned in all the years of college and the classroom was the importance of teachable moments. I discovered early on that I could convey exponentially more information and direction when a child was really tuned in and curious about something I wanted to share than through a whole day of lecturing or doling out homework! Teachable moments matter. If you're a parent, I'm sure you've witnessed this fact as well. Our children are much more apt to listen to what we have to say when they are curious about the subject or when they have had some kind of life affirming or altering event happen to open their eyes to their *need* to listen to what we have to say. Teachable moments…as an educator, I live for them and constantly look for them. You might say that I spend 98% of my time in anticipation of the quality learning that is facilitated in the 2% of time that such moments offer.

Having said all of that, let me drop a small bomb on you. In the spiritual conversations in which we're hoping to engage people, the goal is to create an atmosphere of discipleship. What is discipleship? Well, in its simplest form, it's just teaching people about Jesus. And guess what—the concept of teachable moments applies just as well here as anywhere else. There are times that people are more open to spiritual conversations. There are moments in life when people are more curious about spiritual things. These times may crop up unexpectedly, or we may watch someone's life for a while just knowing that one of these is inevitably going to happen. They come in all shapes and sizes, from the devastating loss of a loved one to something as simple as curiosity kindled when a nonbeliever notices the radical difference made in the life of a Christ-follower. Whatever their nature, during these times the doors for sharing our faith stories are more open than ever.

In these teachable moments, people seem to open their hearts and minds to listen more intently to what we would share with them concerning the hope that is in us. Sometimes we're not prepared for these moments, and we let them slip by without sharing even as much as a single word. This is exactly why Peter encouraged believers to honor Christ as Lord and always be prepared to give an answer to anyone who is curious about the hope that we have within us.[xxiii] Peter encourages us to be ready to share our faith story whenever a door opens to provide such an opportunity. Now, let me add a little something here. While we should always be ready to share as opportunities present themselves, that's really a passive response. I would take this a step further by proposing that in addition to being ready, we should actually *pray* for God to create such opportunities. If these teachable moments provide the best environments for people to listen to, learn from, and respond to the gospel message, doesn't it just make sense that we should constantly be praying for them to happen in the lives of people we know and love?

There have been numerous times throughout the years I've prayed that God would create open doors, God appointed moments, for me to share my faith with people whom I knew needed to hear the gospel message. There have been times that I've been so desperate for others to hear and understand their need for Christ that I've prayed God would do whatever it took to get their attention. Evidently, this was something Paul did as well. In fact, in his letter to the Colossian church, he requests that they join him in praying for open doors. "Devote yourselves to prayer, stay alert in it with thanksgiving. At the same time, pray also for us that God may open a door to us for the message, to speak the mystery of the Messiah-for which I am in prison-so that I may reveal it as I am required to speak."[xxiv]

Notice a few things from this passage. First, Paul tells the church to be devoted to prayer. To be devoted to something means that we are loyal in our involvement in it. Paul is telling Christians that constant prayer will be one of the marks of a faithful follower of Christ. Notice that he also encourages us to remember that thanksgiving is as much a part of the plan as supplication. In the midst of our asking, we must take time to acknowledge God's giving. Going further, Paul requests that, as the Colossian church is asking and thanking, they also ask for God to open doors for the free flow of the gospel. It is important to note also that Paul is clear that God is the one who opens the doors. This is of great importance because many people have been pushed away from Christ, rather than drawn to Him, as Christians have attempted to *force* open doors in order to share the gospel. Instead of forcing our way into the spiritual lives of others, Paul requests that we let God open doors from within.

Think about this for a moment. If you and I constantly try to manipulate circumstances or emotions in order to win someone over to our way of thinking or believing, we come across as pious, bigoted, and condescending. However, if we are simply there to offer encouragement and share our faith stories in the dark hours or curious moments that crop up in the lives of those we love, we exist in a completely different light. This is exactly why I've said from the beginning that a very important goal for us is to have spiritual conversations rather than presentations. Conversations make the most of opportunities while presentations seek simply to make the most opportunities.

You see, God is uniquely suited to create the opportunities His followers need in order to interject truth into the lives of the lost, resulting in their being drawn to Christ rather than pushed away. To be sure, circumstances of life often work together to make people more curious about or open to the message of our faith, but what we must never forget is that it is God who orchestrates the circumstances of life! This means that He is fully capable of opening closed doors, especially in the lives of those He's drawing, to provide His faithful followers the chance to share an answer for the hope which they hold in Christ Jesus.

Perhaps you have been waiting for the right opportunity to share your faith with a coworker, family member, friend, or neighbor that just hasn't come. I would challenge you to begin praying today that God would provide the opportunities for you and others to share with those you know and love. Pray that God would orchestrate the circumstances of lives in such a way that they would be open to the message of hope found in the gospel of Christ, and that, perhaps, they would even be so bold as to *ask* you about your faith. Pray that God would place you into the middle of God appointed moments, teachable moments, where you might share your faith story. Pray that spiritual conversations would happen around you on a daily basis. Pray all of this for yourself and for others. Be devoted in this, praying throughout each day for doors around you to swing open to the gospel of Christ. And when those doors open, jump through them!

PRAYER 4: FOR WORDS TO SAY

One of the biggest fears I have is of looking ignorant. My wife has actually accused me, over the years, of making things up on the spot in order to keep from looking like I don't know something. I will not deny that this very thing has happened, but I will tell you that I try to avoid such a situation at all costs by attempting to know a little bit about a lot of things. This allows me to carry on *seemingly* intelligent conversations with a wide range of folks over various topics. I realize this doesn't sound much better. In fact, you may be judging me right now, but I would remind you that all of us end up in conversations that result in our feeling inadequate at times. When these times happen, you only have a few options. You might jump in with the little bit of knowledge you do have, admitting that you don't know everything on the subject but are curious. You could sit quietly by while everyone else converses. Alternatively, you may choose to leave the conversation altogether.

The reason I bring this up is because if there has ever been a reason that people don't share their faith, it is precisely this: they are worried that they don't have the answers! In other words, they find themselves in that God-appointed moment, but have no idea what to say or how to say it. Perhaps they've been asked a question for which they don't have an answer or to which they have never even contemplated an answer! I'm sure that many of us can identify times in which we've had the perfect opportunity to share the gospel, but have remained silent or left the conversation because we didn't feel adequate to engage the other person in dialogue. If that is you, I want to encourage you with a statement that I've heard many times through the years. When it comes to sharing your faith story, God is not nearly as concerned with your ability to share as He is in your availability to share. Why is that the case? Well, because if you will make yourself available to Him, He will make His power and wisdom available to you.

My father is a self-employed electrician. This means that growing up I enjoyed the wonderful privilege of working with him every summer. I'll admit that as a teenager this was less than a desirable way to spend summers off from school. As I got older, however, I enjoyed the opportunity to join him as it allowed me to reconnect with my childhood and spend some quality time with my dad. Having grown up the son of someone involved in construction, you would probably assume that I have amassed a respectable collection of tools. While this is true, over the years I've come to realize that no matter how many tools one owns, he is always apt to run up on a job that requires a tool he doesn't have! This is always the case when I work with my dad. Though I bring my own tools to the job site, it never fails that some need arises for which I don't have the correct tool. Do you want to know what I do in those moments? Well, I do not just avoid the task. Avoiding the task would mean that the job never gets done. Nor do I just walk off the job and abandon the project. Again, this would leave the goal unaccomplished. I do not stare dumbly, hoping that the correct tool just presents itself. What I do is march out to my father's tool box and borrow one of his! You see, his collection is bigger, better, and more professional than mine. When my tools are inadequate, his are always more than adequate for the job. And, if I'm on the job working alongside him, He's more than willing to share!

I suggest that as we think of spiritual conversations, we need to realize that in the context of communication words are nothing more than tools used to convey meaning. Perhaps the reason you have missed opportunities to share your faith in the past is because you have felt as if you didn't have the right tools for the task. Maybe you have wondered if your tools were adequate. It's quite possible that you've looked at a pastor or evangelist and felt that their tools were more well suited for the job. Has the opportunity ever occurred in which God has thrown the door open for you to share your faith, but rather than dive in headlong, you sat in silence or avoided the opportunity altogether because you didn't feel like you could be successful in sharing? If so, I would encourage you to remember that during those times God has a whole box of tools that He puts at your disposal if you will just trust Him and get to work. In fact, I can't tell you the number of times that I have found myself at a loss for words only to have them supplied in abundance by the power of the Holy Spirit in my time of need.

In another Pauline letter, this time to the church in Ephesus, Paul not only requests that prayers be made for open doors and opportunities, but also that the words he needs to explain the wonder of the cross would be provided to him during his time of need. "Pray also for me," he requests, "that the message may be given to me when I open my mouth to make known with boldness the mystery of the gospel….Pray that I might be bold enough in Him to speak as I should."[xxv] It's important to note the timing of the arrival of these words Paul mentions. Notice that he doesn't request that God let him know far in advance the things he needs to say, as if he would have time to polish them and present them in a more acceptable way. He doesn't even request that the words be supplied immediately before he speaks. His request is that the words would come when his mouth opens. That's kind of waiting to the last minute if you ask me. Paul understands something, however, that you and I have somehow forgotten. When we work alongside God, His intervention follows our investment! If we want God to intervene in our life and the lives of others, then we must obediently invest ourselves in His work!

When we make ourselves available to God, He creates within us an ability to do His work His way! God doesn't need us to lay the foundation for the miracle of salvation to take place. He's already done that at the cross. Furthermore, He is already at work drawing people to Himself and creating open doors for us to share. All of that is His responsibility. Our only responsibilities are to pray that His work would be unhindered and that, as we are obedient to Him, He would provide what we need to fulfill our role in the partnership.

I know you may be reading this and thinking, "Wait a minute. How can I possibly share my faith story when I don't have the theological knowledge I need to do so? Surely, I will get asked a question for which I have no answer!" Well, if that's your position, then I would challenge you with a couple of thoughts. First of all, if you feel uneducated in the area of God's Word, there's no one to blame but yourself! Get out your Bible and start reading. Read the gospels until you have a firm grasp on what they have to say about Christ and our need for Him. Read Paul's letters until you lay hold of the importance of discipleship and the responsibility we have to reach others. If you feel like you don't know enough about the Bible, then read and study the Bible! That's a big "duh," right? Secondly…pray! James 1:5 instructs us in this way: "Now if any of you lacks wisdom, he should ask God, who gives to all generously and without criticizing, and it will be given to him." When we invest ourselves in studying God's Word and request that He quicken our understanding, you better believe that He will honor such work! I'll tell you that there have been times in sharing my faith with others when God has brought to mind passages or answers from Scripture that I did not even know I had learned! Remember that when you partner with God to do His work, He provides the tools!

Let me encourage you with one last thought…our words will never bring anyone to Christ! God's word alone is promised to never return void.[xxvi] Stop relying on your own tools and start making use of God's tools! Remind yourself that when opportunities present themselves, God will give you what you need to make known the power of the gospel. If you will invest, He will intervene. If you will make yourself available, He will make you able! And, like Paul, take it a step further and begin praying now for all those open doors before they present themselves. Pray that in those God moments,

His Spirit would give you the exact words to say and the boldness to say them.

PRAYER 5: FOR EYES TO BE OPENED

I hope you've noticed the progression suggested by these prayers. First of all, we acknowledge that God is the initiator of all relationships, asking Him to draw lost people to Himself. Next, we pray for Christians as a whole to be about the work of God's kingdom. We specifically pray that doors would open and that we would have God-appointed opportunities to share our faith stories with others. We pray that at those moments God would give us the words to say to encourage, invite, and inspire people towards a relationship with Christ. Now, finally, we pray specifically for the understanding and comprehension of those with whom we share. We pray that they would grapple with and grasp the depths of their great need for a Savior!

For as long as I can remember, my family has owned horses. While a lot of my friends had dirt-bikes, three-wheelers, dune buggies, or other powered toys to get them from one end of the woods to the other, I had a horse. My ride had genuine leather upholstery, four-wheel drive, and was cheap on gas! Anyway, I spent a lot of time with our horses and learned a lot about life from dealing with them.

Did you know that sometimes horses get spooked? This isn't usually a good thing, especially if you have some task that you wish for the animal to perform. Over the years, I've seen numerous ways that people have tried to calm down or handle a nervous horse. The twitch is one such devise. It is a chain that raps around the top lip of the horse. When the horse is being unruly, one can tighten this and the horse will stop fighting to avoid the pain it causes. Of course, the effectiveness of this device is determined in great part by the spiritedness of the horse. I've seen horses hobbled to try to get them to remain still. However, if they really get upset, they'll just knock themselves over trying to fight the hobbles. Perhaps the best tool that I have seen used to calm down a horse is the blindfold. A skilled horseman can slip a blindfold over a horse and get him to do almost anything he wants the horse to do simply because he can't see what's going on around him.

I know you're wondering how all this fits within a book about evangelism, but humor me for a moment. If I were a horseman looking for the best way to *fool* a horse into thinking he was safer than he really was in a dangerous situation, the blindfold method would be the one for me. It would make him oblivious to the dangers and problems around him so that he would believe he had no need to fight or flee. He would not realize just what kind of predicament he was in. Now, here's where this hits home for us. There are countless millions in the world today who have been blinded by our enemy the devil to their need for a Savior! They do not realize the perilousness of their situation, apart from Christ. These people go about their lives each day, blinded by their comforts, their financial securities, their lifestyles, even their religions, completely oblivious to their true plight. They just don't see it. In fact, many of them have never even stopped to consider what awaits them in eternity the moment they leave this earth. They are blinded! And the only way they will ever see their need for Christ is if someone removes the blindfold. This is where God comes in.

We've already stated that God draws people to Himself and that He opens doors into people's lives through which the gospel may be delivered. We've even noted that in those moments we should pray that God would give us just the right words to say. There's only one problem; every one of these things may happen, and the gospel still fall on deaf ears if the Holy Spirit of God isn't also working to remove things in a person's life that blind him to his need for Christ.

Oh, how we need a supernatural provision of spiritual sight in this world! I believe that God wants to bring this about! Yet, I would remind you that He will not force Himself into the equation if we refuse to invite Him to act.

Paul talks about the reality of this situation in his second letter to the church at Corinth. The new covenant brought about through the work of Christ on the cross is a glorious and wonderful thing, providing the opportunity for those who were once enemies of God to be adopted as His children. The unbelieving world, however, is unable to see the beauty of the message of the gospel. In fact, Paul states that it is as if there were a veil over the eyes of unbelievers that keeps them from seeing the blatant reality of man's sin, impending condemnation, and available salvation through Christ Jesus. Regarding this, Paul states, "But if, in fact, our gospel is veiled, it is veiled to those who are perishing. Regarding them: the god of this age has blinded the minds of the unbelievers so they cannot see the light of the gospel of the glory of Christ, who is the image of God."[xxvii] According to Paul, unbelievers have been blinded by the devil. Regardless of the makings of the blindfold, humans have not the power to loose and remove it on their own. The purpose of this veil is to keep unbelievers from understanding their need for a Savior. Satan has purposely blinded people so that they will not accept Christ and thus be saved! Our only viable response is to cry out to the Father to counteract this work.

In another letter, this time to the Ephesian church, Paul informs believers that he is praying that God would open the eyes of their hearts, again demonstrating the hopeless state we exist in before the Father does His liberating work in our lives. "I pray," he says, "that the God of our Lord Jesus Christ, the glorious Father, would give you a spirit of wisdom and revelation in the knowledge of Him. I pray that the eyes of your heart may be enlightened so that you may know what is the hope of His calling, what are the glorious riches of His inheritance among the saints, and what is the immeasurable greatness of His power to us who believe, according to the work of His vast strength."xxviii Paul's prayer is that the spiritual eyes of the Ephesians would be opened to see the glorious work of the Father, in the Son, through the power of the Holy Spirit!

I would suggest to you that this is exactly what we should be praying for any who have yet to believe in Christ and especially for those with whom we have relationships. I have felt the frustration of sharing my faith story with others, engaging in spiritual conversations, even of pouring out my heart in hopes that others would call on Christ only to realize that they were wholly incapable of grasping their true predicament. It is a painful thing to want the joy of salvation so badly for those you love only to have them reject it due to their own inability to acknowledge how desperately they are in need of it.

I remember sharing with an exchange student from Germany. Franz had grown up in an Orthodox church where, according to him, the Bible was thought of as little more than a book of stories. No doubt, he had come to believe that it was just such. He had been steeped in the philosophies of secular humanism. He was completely honest with me about his feelings, declaring that humans were nothing more than highly evolved animals. I remember sitting with him for over an hour one night, doing everything I could to help him see the truth of Scripture and the severity of the lies he had bought into. No matter how polished my answers or thorough my explanations, he was not to be won over. I poked holes in his theories and challenged the foundations of his worldviews, but he was unwavering in his determination that Christianity was nothing more than one religious viewpoint in a world of religious viewpoints. I left that encounter discouraged and frustrated because I had done all I knew to do to open his eyes and was wholly incapable.

Today I look back knowing that I was wrong to think my logical arguments and well-thought out presentations could sway him. I saw him as a nut to crack and knew that if I just used a big enough hammer, I could make things happen. The truth, however, is that only God could open his eyes to his need for a Savior. Sadly, I was so confident in my own ability to argue him to Christ that I never asked God to supernaturally remove his spiritual blindfolds. I know that for many people it takes hearing the gospel multiple times before they finally begin to see its truth. I pray that Franz finally did understand and respond in faith to the gospel message. I pray even today that his eyes were opened to His need for Christ.

CONCLUSION

I hope that you come away from this chapter with the comprehension that salvation is a complete and utter work of God. Yes, you and I are agents of the message. We have the privilege of engaging people in conversation and sharing our stories in an attempt to introduce them to Christ. However, it is God—and God alone—who works in one's spirit to draw, to open spiritual eyes, and to convince an individual of his need for Christ. When we make the Great Commitment to pray that believers will be burdened to share, we are praying in harmony with the very heart of God. When we ask Him to open doors so that we might ourselves share our faith stories, we are joining in the work of God. As we pray that He would remove blindfolds and open people's eyes to their need for a Savior, we call upon His power to destroy the strongholds of evil and darkness.

My hope and prayer for you is that you realize the privilege you have been afforded in crying out to the Father for the salvation of the lost. While you and I will never be able to choose Christ on their behalf, we have the responsibility to pray that all hindrances to their free exercise of faith be removed. As you strategically and intentionally pray these 5 things, I encourage you to expect to see God do great things. I challenge you to look for the opportunities that He will provide and take advantage of every teachable moment He offers. Above all, my desire is that you never forget that when God's people invest themselves in His work, God intervenes in their world. Prayer is just such an investment. If you really want to see this world reached with the gospel…if you want to see your friends and family respond to the message of salvation and grace found in Christ…then you must be committed to regular and fervent prayer. Why? Well, because prayer always precedes power!

5

Questions to Ask

By now, I'm sure you've grown accustomed to the contrast between spiritual conversations and presentations. Conversations are powerful and important. Every day you and I have hundreds of different conversations with those around us. These may be in reference to a myriad of topics from work issues to our favorite teams in the weekend football games. Our ability to form words and carry on meaningful dialogue is one of the most distinctive traits of humanity. Animals may travel together, hunt together, and live together, but they don't sit around campfires sharing stories, arguing details, or expounding upon their ideas. Our ability to communicate means that we share more than just space…we share our very selves! Conversation is not only a distinctive human trait but also one of our most powerful tools.

Consider ways I might go about persuading you to think as I do concerning an issue. If I want to win you over to my way of thinking,

I have a few different options available to me. I could physically force you through threat of violence or pain to agree with me or do as I want. While this may initially produce the result that I desire, it's not the best course of action because you may simply be acting or speaking as I wish to avoid pain and suffering. More than likely, I haven't really won you over. In truth, you are probably thinking that as soon as the threat of force is over, you will go back to your original way of thinking or acting.

Another option might be to develop a flashy presentation with alliterated points, illustrations, and a plethora of graphical elements to draw your attention. I could lay all this information out before you in logical format. Once you have all the details, you could make a decision to accept or reject my position. While this approach is better than physical force, it's still not ideal. There is the possibility that, for all my logic, I might miss a point for which you have a serious question. Not only that, but the nature of a presentation puts you in a passive position as the receiver of information while I assume a more active role in disseminating information. Quite honestly, you will not be able to receive and process information as quickly as I'm able to offer it. You may say you accept my stance as proper, but truthfully there is no way for me to know if you really understand everything I've shared. Even if I give you the opportunity to ask questions, so much information is delivered in a presentation that it is quite possible you may forget questions you had at the beginning of our time together.

What if, however, you and I sat down and had a conversation about an issue? Better yet, what if we had a series of conversations, covering different aspects of our topic in each sitting? This dialogue would create opportunities for true meaning to flow between us. You would have the opportunity to articulately establish and thoroughly explain your viewpoint. I could hear what you have to say and respond in turn. Both of us would be active in the pursuit as we work together to understand and come to common ground. Questions would naturally spring up, offering greater opportunities for further exploration and learning. You see, the vehicle of conversation offers us the best tool for ensuring comprehension and informed acceptance.

When it comes to seeking the conversion of others, consider the ways the issue has been handled in the past. There have been times in history when people have forcibly been converted from one religion to another. In fact, that is still the norm among some of the most violent religious groups in the world today. Convert or die is their mantra. Usually, the converts are won out of fear, and if they remain they do so in fear. Are these true converts? I would say no.

In Christian circles, especially in the recent past, we have sought to use the presentation format of conversion. In our minds, if we can just present people with all the facts, they'll see their need for Jesus. This form of evangelism has revealed itself in many ways, with people learning all kinds of acrostics, outlines, and flow charts. I can see a few major problems with this approach in today's world. First of all, America is increasingly becoming a postmodern society. With less emphasis on logical approaches and more attention being given to spatial learning, people find themselves easily lost in the details of a presentation. Another trait of postmodernity is a general lack of respect for authority and distrust of anything that is highly organized. This applies to anyone who would set themselves up as a moral authority or dictator of belief as well. Another characteristic of our times is a general sense of distrust of others. In today's world, it is generally assumed that everyone has an angle. Unless someone has earned trust, folks usually don't accept the validity of what he says even though they may politely listen. For these reasons alone, the presentation method is no longer the most useful tool for sharing one's faith. Just as people avoid a salesman, bent on convincing others of their product's superiority, so people steer clear of religious folks who attempt to "sell" others on their beliefs.

Have you considered a major difference between the first two approaches and conversation? Neither the force approach nor the presentation approach make use of dialogue. That's because both are top-down approaches to bringing about change. The force approach features one who is *physically* stronger imposing his belief system on the weaker while the presentation approach features one who is *intellectually* superior enlightening the uninformed. Both approaches are condescending by nature. Dialogue, however, provides a peer approach rather than a subordinate approach to learning. When I force my ways on you, I do so as a despot. When I present you with facts in an attempt to sway you, I do so as if you are ignorant while I am educated. Both approaches tend toward coldness and are relationally deficient. However, when I engage you in dialogue, I do so as an equal and assume a peer relationship. While I recognize that many have had success over the years with evangelistic presentations, I believe that if we were to closely investigate we'd find that those who have been most successful have always found a way to couch the presentation within conversation.

By its very nature, evangelism is relational. Think about it…you are hoping to lead others into the most important relationship of their entire existence. And, the only reason you are doing so is because you have a relationship with this same great Savior that you're hoping they come to love. Of course, this is only a possibility because the Father desired a relationship with us so much that He sacrificed His Son to make it possible. These truths are exactly the reasons the first two approaches falter: they are not relational.

My suggestion is that we avoid canned presentations altogether and learn what God's Word has to say about salvation and a relationship with Him. Let's engage people in meaningful, intentional dialogue on a daily basis with the goal of moving things in spiritual directions. Let's become as comfortable talking about spiritual things as we are talking about anything else. Let's remind ourselves that our faith is not some set of facts to be memorized, but is rather the very essence of who we are! Let's honestly explore the truth claims of other belief systems. Let's take time to understand them and unpack them. Let's genuinely *listen* to others, so that we might earn the right to be heard ourselves! Let's share our own faith stories, revealing what God has done for us and how He has changed us. Let's take the opportunities that God offers us in conversation to answer for the hope that is in us. Finally, let's do all of this within the context of the relationships that God Himself has provided!

The purpose of this chapter is to give you some tools to do just as I've suggested. Here, you will find questions that you may ask in the course of any conversation that will help steer dialogue in a spiritual direction. These are not meant to be presented as an outline, nor is there any order in which they should be asked. You may discuss them all in one sitting as God provides opportunity, or you may talk through them over the course of days, weeks, or months as "teachable moments" present themselves. You need not even ask the questions exactly as they are written. Perhaps the *meat* of a question is all you will use. Regardless of how you use these questions, I would point out some important things to remember:

- First, remember that evangelism is relational. If you are meeting someone for the first time, unless God just impresses it on your heart, it's probably not a good idea to lead with these questions. Get to know them and give them the opportunity to get to know you!
- Second, constantly remind yourself that these are meant to create opportunities for *dialogue*. Our goal is spiritual conversations, not presentations. Anytime you begin to feel "preachy" or things take on the feel of a lecture, it's time to change the subject.
- Third, let things flow. Don't feel like you need to force the conversation in the direction you want it to go. If you've been

praying, you've already asked God to create the opportunity, to draw the person with whom you're talking, and to give them spiritual insight. Use these questions as feelers to see where people are spiritually and to determine what God is doing. By exploring these questions, you are simply making yourself available for God's use.

- Most importantly, after you ask a question, *be quiet and listen!* By definition, dialogue requires an exchange. Let this happen. One of the wonderful things that may happen is that, as you quietly listen, the other person may invite you to share your feelings on the topic. If this happens, feel free to do so. Otherwise, just listen, asking more questions as needed to better understand the other person's viewpoint. By listening, you're earning an audience for when you want an opportunity to share! Make sure that you thoroughly understand a person's response to these questions before you try to share your own beliefs.

By genuinely listening to the ways people respond, you should be able to accurately determine what their faith views are and how God might be dealing with them. The last question you will ask is for permission to share what you believe. When you get that opportunity, you will actually be letting the Bible do all the talking. In the next chapter, we will discover 5 verses you can share that succinctly convey the truth of the gospel. Remember that the speed at which you move through these questions will be determined by the other person's interest, God's guidance, and your spiritual sensitivity. Don't feel like you must hurry things to a conclusion, but also don't miss doors that God throws open for a decision. By the way, let me reiterate that perhaps the worst thing that could happen would be for you to ask a question and then seem uninterested or impatient as someone responds. Many of us try to formulate our own answer or think ahead to our next point the minute we ask a question. Avoid this reaction! You seriously want to know how others will answer these questions! So, LISTEN!!!

QUESTION 1: ARE YOU A SPIRITUAL PERSON?

This is a pretty safe question with which to begin a spiritual conversation. Many people consider themselves to be spiritual in some way or another. According to a Pew Research study, at least eighty-three percent of people in the United States consider themselves to hold religious beliefs.[xxix] The truth is that whether or not they are willing to admit it, all people have some kind of religious belief system. Even an atheist *believes*…he just believes, spiritually speaking, that there is nothing in which to believe. I know—there is definite irony in that viewpoint. The only caveat here is that we have been conditioned to think in American culture that one's faith is a private issue not to be talked about. By beginning with this question, you are giving the other person permission to share his feelings without the threat of having your beliefs forced on him or having his hand slapped.

Another reason this question is appropriate is because it's a simple request for a person to share an opinion. In other words, inherent in the question is the assumption that, being a request for an opinion, you're not looking for a specific response. Don't be alarmed if the other person gives you some off-the-wall explanation of his faith. Remember that you asked for his opinion, so validate him as an individual even if you fundamentally disagree with his beliefs. Ask questions as needed to assist in completely unpacking the details of his faith system. If you listen closely to how the other person answers this question, you may be able to pick up on whether or not he has a saving faith in Christ right off the bat.

Usually, individuals will be happy to go deeper than just answering with a simple "yes" or "no;" however, if they do not, ask them to explain what makes them spiritual people and what their specific beliefs are. Because we've been conditioned to think faith is a private matter, some folks may need encouragement to really open up. Remember that the purpose of this question is to get the ball rolling. Your desire is to open the door to talk about spiritual things and to create a safe environment for dialogue. Therefore, give others the chance to have the floor and then sit back and listen.

The hardest part of this approach may be controlling your compulsion to call something crazy or poke holes in someone else's views. It is important to remember that we don't have to agree with others in order to listen to and be interested in their viewpoints. In fact, we have many conversations every day with folks who hold differing opinions from us on a host of issues from political leanings to favorite flavors of pizza. Just as these issues rarely affect the validity of a relationship, we may also disagree on issues of faith and still treat others with love and respect. At this point in the conversation, you should be in information processing mode. Don't feel like you need to convince anyone of anything.

An important point to recognize is that you always want to leave the door open to future spiritual conversations. If at all possible, never burn a bridge! Any time you feel that a person is shutting down or getting defensive or argumentative, it's best to change the topic in hopes that you might come back to spirituality again at a later time. Remember that we are working alongside God, asking Him to draw and create opportunities. You should be able to determine pretty quickly whether or not He is at work as you engage others. If you sense that the timing isn't right, then hold off and keep praying for that person. By the way, pray for him *as he shares*! I have asked this question to people before only to have them, as they explain, decide for themselves that their beliefs really don't make sense.

If the person is open to talking to you about his faith and depending on the direction and flow of the conversation, you may choose to move on to another topic or to ask another one of the questions below.

QUESTION 2: WHAT HAPPENS WHEN WE DIE?

The purpose here is to determine if others believe in an afterlife, and if so, what their beliefs entail. There are very few people who think that we simply cease to exist at death. According to a Religion in the Millenial Generation study, seventy-four percent of people believe that there really is life after death.[xxx] For the sake of argument, let's just think about the alternative to this view for a moment. If one believes that a person just ceases to exist when he dies, that belief creates somewhat of a conundrum for living. On the one hand, one would obviously want to make the most of every moment he has because once he's dead, that's it! He would be wise to "eat, drink, and be merry"...after all, tomorrow he may die. On the other hand, such a carefree and reckless lifestyle may actually hasten his impending demise. Generally speaking, those who abuse their bodies don't get as many years out of them as those who take care of them by living a more conservative lifestyle. Obviously, this belief system would create a certain degree of dissonance in one's life. This is precisely why most people accept some kind of religious belief, even if some of their views are a bit far-fetched. These beliefs give meaning and purpose to the time individuals have in life and answer questions about what will happen when that time is up.

Regardless of one's viewpoint, not many enjoy talking about the end of life. Death is a topic that most folks spend their lives trying to avoid. The truth, however, is that it can't be avoided forever! I spend a lot of time with teenagers. Teens as a whole hate to talk about death. In fact, if you want to see a whole room of teenagers get deathly quiet, just tell them that death is the topic of conversation for the evening. This is understandable as in their minds they have their whole lives in front of them. This belief is precisely the reason the passing of a young person is so devastating. When a young person dies, we all feel the burden of potential lost. So, while many people may feel completely comfortable discussing their faith, the issue of death may make them feel a bit uneasy. Discomfort, however, is completely acceptable in this case as it means that there is an underlying issue that perhaps hasn't been resolved. Expect the tension and meet it with complete trust in the Lord.

As your friend responds to this issue, you must be sure not to rush him to supply an answer. The question may create an awkward silence. One of the things I often tell folks is that Christians must embrace awkwardness if we want to be faithful to Jesus. So, if an awkward silence results from asking this question, embrace it rather than trying to fill it. More than likely, no response means that the other person is processing what they believe or how they feel. Perhaps they have recently lost a loved one so this topic feels very raw to them. You may actually discover an opportunity to minister to them in their time of pain or grief. It may be a perfect time to talk about the issue. I've seen some of the worst heathens develop a sudden interest in spiritual things precisely because someone close to them had passed on.

Another possibility is that the person has really never considered the issue before. Remember that most people do all they can to push the thought of death to the backs of their minds. Maybe your friend is considering his views based on what he shared concerning his beliefs. Perhaps his current belief system doesn't satisfactorily answer questions about death. In addition, there could be an inconsistency between what he believes and what he actually feels. Again, we've prayed that God would draw and open eyes to areas of blindness.

Let your friend wrestle with his answer because this is a question for which an answer is worth the wait.

You may find that after people share, they might ask you what you believe about life after death. They may also ask you to share your beliefs if they are unsure how to answer the question themselves. Feel free to share, but keep it simple. Perhaps mention that you believe you will spend eternity with God, but don't go too deeply into this as you run the risk of having them mimic your answer, especially if they don't have answers of their own. Also, giving too much of an answer here may color the responses they give to other questions you may ask later on. Remember that the questions are tools designed to help you determine where others are spiritually. Until you have a good idea of where people stand, it would be beneficial to remain a bit vague in your feedback. You want to be very careful not to influence their honest opinions. Obviously, if they have a real saving faith in Christ, they should have already processed most of these issues and have fairly concrete answers. You will eventually provide answers as well, but you need to be very careful in the course of this dialogue not to *help* others answer your questions!

As you explore this issue with them, it may also be a good time to ask if they believe that a person has a soul or spirit, and if so, what happens to it when a person dies. Another great follow-up would be to ask them to share their thoughts on heaven and hell. Once you get them to talking, expect that their answers may be pretty different from your own. They may talk about spiritism, ghosts, or reincarnation. Maybe they believe that we have a life-force that joins a greater energy or force when we die. They may reveal that they believe in a universal form of salvation or that where one spends eternity is based on works or deeds. Some folks believe that it is possible for people to become angels, looking out for those whom they've left behind. They may actually shock you and talk about the importance of a relationship with God. Again, listen for clues as they talk, knowing that according to Jesus the only way to heaven is through a relationship with Him.[xxxi] If they offer any other alternative, chances are pretty good that you're talking with someone who is in serious need of Christ.

Death demands that we consider the possibility that there may be more to life than just what is in front of us. Being such a deep issue, you may find that this dialogue becomes a major turning point in your conversations. Having shared something so personal, they may feel much more at ease when you bring up other questions pertaining to spirituality. Not only that, as they become more comfortable with the fact that you aren't going to judge their worth, based on their having a different view, you earn credibility and your relationship will actually deepen. At any rate, once you feel like you have a good understanding of their beliefs on this topic, move on to another question, change the subject, or agree to talk again soon. Remember that the goal is to leave the door open to future spiritual conversations, not to push someone into a decision they're not ready to make. If someone is obviously interested in your beliefs, it is a good chance that God is working with him. Feel free to take the opportunity to ask more questions and go deeper. Curiosity may have killed the cat, but it has also been the catalyst for many to come to know Jesus.

QUESTION 3: WHAT ARE YOUR THOUGHTS ON GOD?

This question moves us a little closer to nailing down a person's understanding of Biblical truth and whether or not he believes what Scripture says about God. The truth is that most people believe that there is a God. Those choosing not to believe in God make up a minority of the world's population. In fact, in a 2012 Pew Research

Center study, only 2.4% of Americans identified themselves as atheists.^{xxxii}

While the majority of people do believe in God, there is a wide range of opinions on who or what He is. Agnostics believe that while there may be a God, He is unknowable, distant, unreachable, or irrelevant. Some hold religious views that describe God more as a spiritual force or energy. Others believe that God is in all things and that all things are part of God. Every organized religion worships its own form of deity. Some of these are polytheistic, meaning they worship multiple gods, while monotheistic religions like Judaism, Islam, and Christianity each worship single divine beings that, on the surface, appear similar. However, we must make no mistake in assuming that these three groups worship the same God, only in different ways! The God of Christianity is unlike any other in all the universe. All of this is to say that when you ask someone if he believes in God, you may be surprised by their answer.

As you listen, don't be too quick to assume that folks are believers just because their view of God sounds a bit biblical. Remember that there is a huge difference between knowing about someone and knowing someone…especially when it comes to God. It is quite common for people to grow up in a Christian environment having believing friends or family. They may have learned how to use Christian terminology or adopted a view of God that sounds orthodox on the surface but has little power or effect in their lives. Many people's views of God paint Him more as a cosmic genie or granter of personal favors than the all knowing designer and planner of the universe. Be sure to take as much time as possible leading them to fully explain their views of God and how those views affect their lives.

While we're on the subject, be careful not to assume that someone is a believer just because he tells you he's been baptized or said a prayer.

A relationship with Christ is just that…a relationship! The sincerity of our faith is not determined by the things we do but rather *whose* we are! It is quite possible that many have been led to believe that salvation is a matter of works, even if the works are as simple as a prayer, walking an aisle, or undergoing baptism. I'm not saying those things aren't important, but I want to be clear that relying on any *act* we do for salvation isn't biblical faith! Scripture is crystal clear that salvation is a product of a relationship with Christ that is predicated on a life-altering faith in Christ.

As you progress, bring Jesus into the conversation, asking others what they believe about Him. You may be pleasantly surprised to hear that they believe He is God's Son, sent to die for their sins, and that they have a vibrant relationship with Him. However, you may get some very different answers as well. Remember not to react negatively or defensively as others share. Ask more questions, as needed, to fully understand how they view Jesus. Do they believe that Jesus is God? Was He a prophet, teacher, or something more? Why did He come to earth? What was He trying to accomplish? Where is Jesus now? Do they consider Jesus to be the Son of God? As you listen, rely on the Holy Spirit to guide you in asking more questions. Your goal is to find out what they believe, but you may also find opportunities to ask questions that force them to rethink some of their false notions about Christ.

Realize that some don't see the Holy Spirit as an actual person of the Trinity. Rather, they may see Him as an esoteric or ambiguous force or power that extends from God. Some who seem to have an otherwise authentic belief in God may have a view of the Spirit that is completely inadequate. One role of the Holy Spirit is to connect us to the Father. We often say that "Jesus lives in the heart" of one who is saved. This is not biblically accurate. Scripture tells us that Jesus is currently at the right hand of the Father in heaven.[xxxiii] It is God's Holy Spirit who takes up residence in our souls when we are joined to God in salvation. He acts as our counselor, convicts us of error, and guides us into righteousness.

One thing I have found over the years is that some people *choose* to hold a wrong view of God precisely because of something in their past. Perhaps some unspeakable thing happened to them which caused them to question God's power over life. They may doubt that God has an authentic love for them. Perhaps someone close to them died or suffered and they felt that their prayers went unanswered. Some find it hard to reconcile the idea of a loving God with the fact that, at some point in their lives, God has unmistakably answered "no" to a request that was dear to their hearts. Others have a difficult time reconciling the parallel, yet competing, concepts of a loving God and the prevalence of evil and suffering in the world. Any of these issues and a whole host more may come up as people answer this question. These concerns are often accompanied by strong emotions which may find vent in your conversation. Be sympathetic, demonstrating genuine concern and a desire to hear them out on the subject.

You should not find it very difficult to determine if those you talk to are true believers once this question has been asked. Scripture is very clear that God is sovereignly in control of all things in this world and that He is powerful, loving, just, and true. Scripture teaches that Jesus Christ is one hundred percent God and that all things have been created by Him, through the power of God's Holy Spirit. Jesus Himself claimed to be the Messiah, sent by God for the salvation of mankind through His death, burial, and resurrection. In addition, Christ made it clear that He is the only way to have a relationship with the Father. He demonstrated His deity through miracles and the fulfillment of prophecy. He spoke openly of His desire for meaningful and intimate relationships with people who would trust Him in faith. He suffered and died for sin, rising on the third day. He presently reigns as the sovereign ruler of all things at the right hand of the Father in heaven. He will eventually return to destroy evil, suffering, and death for all time, and to usher in a new creation in which those He has redeemed will spend eternity in fellowship with Him.

If you find that your loved one is a true believer in Christ, celebrate with him the joy found only in Jesus. Realize that though you may no longer need to lead him into a relationship with Christ, spiritual conversations should remain a staple of your relationship. Encourage him to live a life that points others to Christ and to join you in reaching others with the gospel's message of hope.

If your friend expresses viewpoints different from those above then you can feel pretty confident that he is not a believer. Hopefully, you have already been praying for him as he shared with you. Continue to pray that God would open his eyes to his need for Christ and quicken his understanding and that he would be open and curious about your views. If he asks you to share what you believe at this point, you may choose to skip the remainder of the questions and jump right into the truth of the gospel as presented through Scripture. If time doesn't permit for you to move on or if his tone has changed, talk about something else or politely end the conversation for now. Otherwise, you may lead him to explore the only barrier that exists to a true and fulfilling relationship with God by asking the next question.

QUESTION 4: WHAT IS SIN?

The topic of sin can be a touchy subject for some. To be sure, it's a topic that makes all of us a little uncomfortable. We don't like to be reminded of our failures and surely do not want others pointing out our shortcomings…especially if we feel that they have some of their own. The sensitivity of the subject has made a frank discussion about sin and its outcome a sometimes contentious and tense endeavor. There are those who would go so far as to say that real sin doesn't exist but is rather the product of an outdated moral construct based on a Judeo-Christian worldview. These would claim that, as citizens of a postmodern world and notedly post-Christian as well, we are no longer in need of such archaic methods for providing societal norms.

Others would say that there really is no absolute standard of morality. Secularists might argue that as living things evolve, so must the social norms that determine right and wrong. According to these, every person must choose what is right for himself based on the context or situation. "Situational ethics," as this has come to be known, has been around for a long time and has come to be a prevalent mind-set in Western thinking. Anytime you find others attempting to *justify* some wrong they have done, they are applying the rule of situational ethics. The fact is that we are all guilty of this at times. For example, how many times have we told "white lies" because we reasoned that the truth would be too damaging? While we've been taught that lying is wrong, we knowingly do it to avoid conflict or pain. Have you ever taken something that didn't belong to you, even something of the smallest value, because you reasoned that it would never be missed, that you needed it worse than the original owner, or that it was just going to be wasted anyway? Situational ethics has become an accepted and expected part of American society. The concept has been taken so far that many have begun to believe that if there is a good enough reason for doing something, then it really can't be wrong at all.

If the concept of situational ethics allows leeway in justifying our sin, the advent of moral relativism has provided complete freedom to do whatever feels right…whenever it feels right…without any justification whatsoever! The mantra here is "if it feels right then do it!" Moral relativism does away with the need to defend our wrong-doing by telling us that right and wrong are relative not only to circumstances but also to individuals interpreting the circumstances. In other words, there really is no need to justify your actions because no one else can really say that what you do is wrong anyway. This philosophy is individualism taken to the greatest extreme. Holders of this viewpoint would claim that what is right for them is right for them and what is right for you is right for you. This understanding puts all moral viewpoints on equal ground; therefore, all morality is relative. This being the case, you don't have a right to hold me to your standards any more than I have a right to hold you to my own. Not only is this a dangerous view to live by, but it is incredibly destructive to the longevity of any society that embraces it. Imagine the chaos and anarchy that would ensue if this way of thinking were adopted on a wide-scale.

While many people make decisions about right and wrong based on how issues make them feel, Christianity, on the other hand, bases right and wrong on what the absolute truth of God's word says regardless of feelings. God's standard is extrinsic to us. In other words, we don't define sin; God does! As believers, we find this truth to be incredibly comforting. I don't have to spend time wrestling with whether or not I *feel* something is wrong. I simply hold it up to God's Word and allow His truth to inform my decision. Now, while we may find it comforting to move out of the moral driver's seat of our lives, non-believers often feel just the opposite. It is threatening to others who have no relationship with God to think that He would impose His will and ways on them. What's more intimidating is the idea that this God intends to judge them based on His standard whether they agree to it or not. This understanding of God's judgment is exactly what leads some to wholly discount the very existence of the concepts of sin and absolute morality.

As you listen to the answers to this question, keep these different viewpoints in mind. Try to determine which of these is closest to the perspective held by your friend. Understanding this answer will go a long way towards helping you process how to discuss his need for a Savior. Obviously, if he doesn't believe that sin is a real thing, then you've got some more talking to do when you get to that subject later on. If he believes that sin is real but that he is somehow morally superior to those around him, then you'll want to make sure you address that viewpoint as well. This is another one of those times when you will want to make special efforts not to be argumentative but inquisitive.

Let's be honest about something: until one realizes the gravity of his sinfulness, he is not ready to recognize his need for a Savior. As you ask probing questions, keep this fact in mind. By asking the right questions and allowing your friend to talk, you may be providing a forum or atmosphere for him to self-explore an issue that most of us spend a good bit of effort avoiding. As you partner with God in this endeavor, remember that there is a great possibility that He has already been working in your friend's heart to convince him of his depravity. Perhaps your friend has built up all kinds of arguments to assure himself of his innate goodness. As he seeks to answer this question, some of those arguments may be challenged.

QUESTION 5: MAY I SHARE WHAT I BELIEVE?

As stated before, there is a possibility that you may never even get to ask this question. As you sit and listen to others' responses to questions, they may demand more and more from you in the way of your own answers. If that is the case, then you should happily follow the Spirit's leadership in sharing from the Bible concerning your own belief system. If, however, you've been patiently listening over the course of minutes, weeks, or months to the answers your friends been offering, this is the moment you've been waiting for. In fact, part of the reason you have listened so attentively is so that you might earn an audience. You see, for the most part, when people feel like they have been heard, they are much more willing and ready to listen to what others have to say. This is precisely why I have encouraged you over and over to *listen* without feeling like you need to set folks straight or interject your own opinions. You have been earning the right to be heard! There are a few possible responses to this question.

There is a chance that though you have listened with all your heart to every response, your loved one may not want to hear what you have to say. If one tells you that he is uninterested, then I would suggest simply sitting quietly. By listening, you've earned the right to participate in the conversation. For your friend to refuse your contribution creates a one-sided situation...let this reality resonate. Silence is awkward, but it also provides an opportunity for people to process. "Wait time" is a wonderful tool that many great educators incorporate in their classrooms. We often move on from things too soon because we are uncomfortable with the silence that staying on topic produces. Your friend may actually expect for you to share without permission, hoping this would give him an excuse to argue or leave the conversation. Don't bite! It is very important that you have permission before you move forward. His reluctance to let you share may simply be a stall tactic or a front to mask inner conflict. Your friend may very well be surprised that you are willing to leave off without sharing your viewpoint and subsequently reconsider his answer. Wait him out and see if he changes his mind. If he does, then you're all set to share from Scripture what you believe!

If your friend remains unwilling to hear you, you should let him change the topic and move on to other things. Remember that one of our main goals is to never burn bridges, but to always leave lines of communication open for future opportunities. Perhaps the timing is not right for you to move further in conversation with him. Remember that we are working alongside God and that He is the one who draws people to Himself. He alone is capable of removing blinders so that people may see their need for Him. It is the Spirit of God who works within people to soften hearts to the message of the gospel. Don't be discouraged! Trust that God will reward your efforts by continuing to work even after you've left the conversation. Days or weeks later, your friend may come back to you and ask you to share, having had more time to think and become curious about your answers to these questions. Regardless, never *force* yourself on others as that may simply push them further away. Continue to pray for your friend and look for opportunities to have other spiritual conversations. When possible, come back to this one. Eventually you very well could get your chance! Each time you demonstrate respect for others' boundaries, you earn a bit more the right to be heard.

Of course, the answer you are hoping to hear is that others would love to hear your thoughts on these questions. If that happens to be the case, then there are a couple of things you'll need to share with them before moving on. First, reveal to them (if they don't already know) that you are a follower of Christ and that your relationship with Him has affected every area of your life. Let them know that as a follower of Christ the Bible informs all of your decisions and gives you answers to all of life's most important questions. This being the case, you will be sharing your perspective with them but using God's words to do so. That's right, the answers to these questions are all found in the Bible.

You might wonder why we'll use Scripture to answer these questions. Well, let's be honest about the fact that your words…and my words as well…carry very little weight or authority. However, God's words carry all authority! When He speaks, every syllable carries the same power as those that spoke an entire universe into existence. Listen to what God has to say about His words: "For just as rain and snow fall from heaven, and do not return there without saturating the earth, and making it germinate and sprout, and providing seed to sow and food to eat, so My word that comes from My mouth will not return empty, but it will accomplish what I please, and will prosper in what

I send it to do."[xxxiv] Therefore, as we have the opportunity to answer these great questions, we'll not waste time or breath using our feeble words but will go straight to the words of God Himself.

CONCLUSION

If I could remind you of one thing it would be this: the approach to evangelism we are exploring is not a program or a process. This approach is only effective within the context of genuine relationship. Relationships take time, effort, and intentionality! You can't "fake" your way through listening with the hope that you'll be allowed to finally share. You will come across as hypocritical at best or manipulative at the worst. Engage others in genuine conversation, demonstrating an honest interest in their beliefs and values. You want them to honestly listen to and investigate your views after all!

Another thing to remember is that the goal of this approach is to have spiritual conversations, not presentations or lectures. When conversation ceases, it's time to move on to something else. Constantly build relational bridges by listening and doing everything in your power to preserve those access points for future use. One thing you will definitely find is that as you get to know another person better, spiritually speaking, the depth of your relationship will improve as a byproduct. You're not just hearing what they believe, you're learning what makes them tick. You are also practicing valuable communication skills that can be applied in all other areas of your friendship!

It is of utmost importance during this time of listening that you have spiritual ears. Obviously, you will pick up on many clues about the spiritual life of the person with whom you're talking. As you listen, pray! When you hear things that surprise you or cause you to be concerned, pray! When a question is asked of you, pray before you answer. If you've done your homework, you've been praying that God would open your friend's eyes to see his need for a Savior, you've been praying for an opportunity to share, and you've been praying that God would draw your friend to Himself. Don't stop praying now! By the time this portion of the conversation is over, you should have a very good understanding of where your friend stands with Christ. If this is an ongoing conversation, you will know a little better after every series of talks how to pray for God to work with your friend. As you listen with spiritual ears, the Holy Spirit will guide your prayers and your responses.

When you first begin to ask these kinds of questions, things may feel unnatural. Don't be alarmed by this and don't give up. I am convinced that part of the reason many people do not share their faith stories with those around them is because they are afraid it will make their relationships awkward. The truth is that, at least initially, it may do just that. Of course, discomfort will only be multiplied by a lack of good listening or falsely feigned interest. Expect the awkwardness and embrace it. You may find that moving through the awkwardness together creates a certain degree of trust. Be encouraged with the knowledge that Christ often embraced difficult situations for the glory of the Father. Perhaps He is calling us to do the same.

Every day you and I have hundreds of conversations with dozens of people. The majority of these deal with issues surrounding jobs, families, friendships, and a plethora of other topics. What if, however, we began to intentionally engage in opportunities for spiritual dialogue? What if we made it a goal to test the waters of what God might be doing on a daily basis by seeking to explore the spiritual lives of those whom He has placed in our lives? My prayer is that you have learned some very useful tools to turn almost any conversation in a spiritual direction. The truth is that these suggestions are just a starting point. Once you become more comfortable with talking about these kinds of things in your relationships, I'm sure you will find a variety of other ways to get the ball rolling in a spiritual direction.

One last thing…enjoy this! Getting to know someone else should be a delightful adventure. This adventure should be made all the sweeter by the knowledge that you are praying for and hoping for the eternal joy of your loved one. Listen attentively. Engage with exuberance. Let the love of Christ flow through you. Allow His patience and mercy to reign in you. Let the Holy Spirit guide you. Be bold, but humble! Demonstrate courage with compassion! Seek understanding and pray for the understanding of your friend. And, once you've done all these things, enthusiastically share an answer for the hope within you!

5

Verses to Share

Not long ago, a major hotel chain ran a series of commercials in which a person was seen completing some heroic or noteworthy endeavor. In one episode we were introduced to a man who solved a great equation that had stumped the greatest minds in history. Another feature depicted a man heroically performing surgery to save someone's life, while yet another introduced us to a guy who stepped in to stop a meltdown at a nuclear power plant. In each episode, the hook came when the characters revealed that they weren't really who everyone thought they were. They had no experience, degree, or expertise in the areas for which they were receiving acclaim. Their amazing abilities were simply the result of having stayed in this specific hotel chain the night before. The idea is that a good night's sleep at this hotel makes one smarter and more prepared to take on the day.

If only it were as easy to attain credibility and knowledge as sleeping at just the right hotel. The truth is that many of us spend years working or studying without ever being recognized as authorities or experts in our fields. This is precisely why we often appeal to someone who is perceived to be greater than us when we make a claim or attempt to support an idea. We do this because we recognize that people do not necessarily respect our authority on issues. I would posit that such is definitely the case when it comes to words that are meant to alter someone's life and eternity in response to Christ as well. Our words simply do not have the power to call someone to radical repentance and obedience. While it is vastly important that we share our faith stories and openly talk about what Christ has done in and for us, I would suggest a different approach when it comes to convincing someone else of the need for Christ.

We live in a world where all the greatest things are polished, packaged, and presented in nice little bundles that sparkle and shine. This tactic has led many to believe that the best way to "sell" the gospel is to boil it down to the basics, polish it up with a nice acronym and a few catch phrases, and package it in a nice tract or program, complete with a "repeat after me" prayer to be learned and reproduced. While this approach is certainly tempting, I have repeatedly suggested that it's not the most productive way for people to be introduced to the gospel message. For years I used these tools to try to lead others to Christ. However, I've learned that while not necessarily bad, starting with our words and moving to Scripture is a backwards approach. The truth is that Christ doesn't need me to interpret His words for Him. If the Holy Spirit is working in someone's heart, He is more than able to quicken that person's understanding of Scripture when he reads it. In fact, Christendom is full of stories of people who just picked up a Bible, began reading, became convicted of their need for Jesus, confessed Him as Lord, and believed on Him in faith. Therefore, I propose that the best course is to start with God's words, not our own. In so doing, we

appeal to a greater authority in talking with others about Christ...
the authority of Scripture.

While our words may carry emotional or logical weight, God's
words are spiritually powerful and authoritative, capable of affecting
the deepest core of a person's being.[xxxv] When God's Word is sown
in the fertile soil of someone's heart it takes on a life of its own,
producing fruit.[xxxvi] As we pointed out in the last chapter, it was God
Himself who said that His Word will never return to Him empty
but will accomplish what He pleases and prosper in what He sends it
to do.[xxxvii] I don't know about your words, but I know that this isn't
true of my own. I may argue and attempt to convince with little or
no success. Just ask my wife! It is precisely because of the weakness of
my own words that, when given permission to share what I believe, I
lead with God's Word and follow with my own rather than the other
way around. I may have but one chance to present truth to the one
I care about. I don't want to waste even a moment of that time with
words that have no power.

Throughout this book, I've suggested that this approach to
evangelism leverages relationality. Think about how you might go
about introducing a friend to someone new. You may begin by telling
your friend about the person to whom you want to introduce them.
You may share how the relationship with this other person has been
a blessing to you. There comes a point, however, when your words
aren't enough to accomplish the building of a relationship between
these two. What must happen is a meeting. Furthermore, while
you may arrange the meeting and make the initial introductions,
you must eventually fade into the background and allow your two
friends to have a conversation of their own. It is only through a one-
on-one conversation that your friends will connect and move past
mere acquaintance to relationship. This situation is precisely what
needs to happen as we seek to lead others to Christ. There must be

a point at which we fade into the background and allow Christ to do the talking through His Word.

I want to reiterate that I believe our faith stories are important and that we should talk openly of them, but when we have the fragile and fleeting opportunity to share the beauty of the gospel, I believe it's best to let Scripture do the talking. For this reason, in this chapter I will suggest 5 verses that clearly illustrate the default state of humanity as condemned, explain what God has done to justify and redeem us, and reveal what our proper response must be in order to experience the grace He offers. However, let me make some suggestions before we go any further:

- Remember that God's Word has complete authority; therefore, we will allow Scripture to do the talking. You will find yourself occupying the role of listener and guide as you engage your friends and ascertain their grasp of Scripture's truth.
- The ideal situation would include your friends' actually reading Scripture out loud for themselves rather than your reading it to them. When they listen to you, they engage the text with one faculty — hearing. However, when they read the text aloud, they are interacting with the text through multiple senses, allowing for a greater understanding and less chance for distraction or inattentiveness.
- The great news is that since you'll have them read the passages, you don't have to memorize verses! You only need to remember where to find the passages. In fact, you may want to simply mark your Bible to make finding a passage easier. Obviously, this means that you need to have a Bible (or Bible app) with you at all times.
- After your loved one reads each passage, you should ask him what he understands it to say. While each falls under one of 5 section headings, I do not expect that you will share

these. These are only there to provide a frame of reference for you to be confident in your understanding of the "meat" of each passage. If the person is clear about the meaning of the passage, move on to the next one. If he is unsure or misunderstands completely, spend some time explaining the truth that the passage is trying to convey or asking questions that lead him in a direction that will allow self-discovery of the truth. Obviously, you are going to be praying the 5 prayers we've talked about as you guide.

- One last thing...remember that this is a conversation. Once Scripture has been read, feel free to take as much time as needed to thoroughly discuss the meaning of the passage and its implications on humanity. God may choose to work through this conversation to convince the other person of his desperate need for a relationship with the Father through His Son.

I hope you have begun to understand something that should provide you with a great measure of relief. Since God will be doing most of the talking through His Word, there is little for you to mess up! Your number one priority is to get God's Word before your friend and then to ease back and let the Holy Spirit work in his heart. I'm not saying that you're completely off the hook, but you definitely have a much smaller responsibility than if the entire conveyance of the gospel depended on your ability to memorize, regurgitate, and give an explanation of the facts of a presentation! This should take much of the fear and anxiety out of sharing your faith. If someone doesn't like what he's hearing, it's God's Word with which he takes issue, not you!

One last thing before we get to the passages. Unlike the questions we looked at in the last chapter, the order of these verses is very important. There is a logical progression to the truth they convey. In addition, it would be best to have your friend explore all of them in one sitting. While the conversation up to this point may have taken thirty minutes or may have happened over the course of weeks or months, this is a time when you will not want to be interrupted or sidetracked. Do everything in your power to effectively block off the time for your friend to adequately explore the claims made by Scripture. If time doesn't allow for this, it may be best to schedule another meeting to continue the conversation. Remember that if at any time your friend decides the conversation is over, your responsibility is to honor this wish and pray for another opportunity. All of that being said, let's look at 5 verses that clearly explain the truth of the gospel.

VERSE 1: GOD IS HOLY

> *"For God's wrath is revealed from heaven against all godlessness and unrighteousness of people who by their unrighteousness suppress the truth, since what can be known about God is evident among them. From the creation of the world His invisible attributes, that is, His eternal power and divine nature, have been clearly seen, being understood through what He has made. As a result, people are without excuse."Romans 1:18-20*

God is. No doubt, some disagree with this point. However, the truth is that no human argument, no matter how convincing, can adequately disprove the existence of God. Even in light of the most well thought out objections to His existence, the fact that God is greater than anything humanity can fully comprehend means that He would continue to exist even if *no one* believed! Let me illustrate this point.

Imagine an unreached tribe of people in the deepest parts of the jungles of South America. These folks have had little, if any, contact with the rest of the world, thus their knowledge of the outside world is incomplete. Now, imagine that you were someone stranded in this jungle and happened upon this group who graciously took you in. As you share with them the wonders of the world—automobiles, skyscrapers, electricity, air travel, space ships, etc—I'm sure they would find it quite unbelievable. In fact, they may violently disagree, thinking you to be mad! Does their lack of knowledge negate the existence of these things? Of course not! If they choose not to believe your report, do those things cease to exist? By no means! The same truth applies to modern man when it comes to God.

Many would say that there is no proof of God's existence, or at least no proof that would suffice for them. However, just because folks don't recognize the evidence doesn't necessarily mean that He's not there. It is virtually impossible to prove the nonexistence of anything unless one is capable of being in all places at all times to ensure the thing doesn't exist in an area of which one knows nothing about. You see, I don't *believe* that unicorns exist, but I can't actually prove that they don't! To claim that God doesn't exist is more of a faith statement than an admission of fact. On the other hand, in order to prove plausible existence, one only needs one or two good pieces of evidence. If I come across just a few pieces of solid evidence that there actually are unicorns, it will require me to reevaluate my beliefs concerning their existence. So, unless someone is capable of knowing all things, it is quite impossible to prove the nonexistence of God as it is plausible that He does in fact exist as part of knowledge the person has not yet been exposed to or attained. Furthermore, there is a whole world of evidence pointing in favor of His actual existence! In other words, people's complaints over lack of sufficient evidence for God doesn't speak to the issue of His existence nearly as much as it speaks to the issue of their ignorance. Thinking about this issue from a logical perspective provides that it's not only possible, but quite plausible that God really does exist. In fact, it actually requires more faith to believe He doesn't exist than that He does! At the very least, His nonexistence is impossible to prove. Therefore, God is!

To simply assume that God *is* doesn't quite go far enough, however. To be thorough we must also confess that God *is holy*! In other words, He's in a class by Himself. If we assume the existence of God, we must also assume that He is not like us. The truth is that there is no one who can compare to God, and being the creator of all things means that all truth is defined by the character of His being. The first pages of the Bible clarify and illustrate this understanding. The writer of the book of James says that God is the author and benevolent giver of all good things.[xxxviii] There is no good thing in this world, no blessing or joy, that has not found its ultimate genesis in Him. All good and wonderful things in this life point us back to the Author of life. King David wrote about God's magnificence in Psalm 8, declaring that the reality of God's goodness causes him to wonder what man has done to deserve the blessings He so willingly pours out. Again, in Psalm 33 the Psalmist praises God for His creative power, righteousness, deliverance, protection, and provision, claiming that his hope is in the Lord alone. He is a holy, just, good, loving, and merciful God for whom there is no equal in all of eternity!

Some people claim that the presence of evil in this world is a solid case against the existence of a good, loving, and benevolent God. Their argument is that a good, loving, all-powerful God would not allow the kinds of evil to exist in the world that we see today. I would suggest two things in response to this view.

First, if this good, loving, all-powerful God does not exist, then where do we get our frame of reference for what is evil or good in the first place? Think about this with me. If I have no perfect standard of good, how can I ever truly know that something *isn't* good. If God doesn't exist, then the default state of all mankind *must* be moral relativism! If mankind determines what is considered good or not good, then every individual has the right to redefine the terms as each sees fit. In other words, by appealing to the concept of evil as evidence against God, folks unintentionally support the idea of a being greater than themselves who determines what evil actually is. You see, if God didn't exist, rather than a universal valuing of life, joy, and happiness, we would expect to see whole societies where murder is welcomed as a good thing, theft is encouraged, abuse is enjoyed and welcomed, and starvation, hunger, and exposure are viewed as blessings. The fact that there is a universal desire for happiness, justice, fairness, and equality proves that there is a standard greater than humanity. This standard is defined by the character of God!

Secondly, the existence of evil in this world is not as much an argument against God as it is an indictment against humanity. To look at this from the standpoint of an atheist, let's assume there is no God. Now, how does one account for evil in the world? I can see two ways one might answer this question. Some may say that evil is just a moral construct; therefore, it doesn't really exist. In other words, something is only evil if it causes us discomfort or creates hardship. If this is the case, then where does evil find its source? No doubt, within humanity. People commit evil acts, harming others and adding to the pain and suffering in this world. Others might say that since humans are just animals our perception of evil is really based on how things affect our homeostasis, environment, or habitat. This viewpoint again begs us to answer the question of where these things find their ultimate source. Obviously, the majority of evil would find its source in humanity while other sources might be nature, society, culture, or even the animal kingdom. If you were to have a conversation with many die-hard naturalists, you would pick up on this sentiment exactly…namely that humans are parasites that are ruining this world with their violence, pollution, and selfishness. So regardless of how one looks at the issue of evil, with or without God we still have to answer the question of the source of pain, suffering, and evil. And the answer is painfully simple: evil comes from us!

I believe the existence of evil in no way impinges upon the reality of God. In fact, it actually creates a basis for understanding what true good is and, therefore, points us to the very nature of God. Not only that, I would suggest that the source of evil remains the same with or without a belief in God: the source is mankind! We are the source of all things evil, while God is the source of all things good. This understanding, in essence, is what we mean when we say that God is holy! God is completely different from us. Within His nature there is no possibility of sin, injustice, unfairness, or evil. In fact, His nature is what serves as our definition of sin. Scripture tells us that God is the same yesterday, today, and forever.[xxxix] Have you ever stopped to consider that the unchanging nature of God is precisely why there is a vast agreement in areas of morality all over the world regardless of race, culture, or religion? Humanity's universal understanding of right and wrong exists precisely because a holy God has written His laws on our hearts. He has hardwired them into our very being. This is why there is no excuse for anyone who lives a sinful life. As my mother says, "They know better."

God's holiness is affirmed throughout Scripture. Perhaps two of the greatest passages illustrating this fact are found in Isaiah six and Revelation four. In both, we see a glimpse into the throne room of heaven. We are told that God sits on His throne surrounded by worshippers, specifically living creatures who never stop saying, "Holy, holy, holy, Lord God, the Almighty, who was, who is, and who is coming." Even as you sit and read this, these words are being uttered over and over again in heaven. The worship of God and the declaration of His holiness are ongoing, ever-present realities in eternity. In biblical language, any word spoken three times signifies completeness. By declaring that God is "holy, holy, holy," these creatures are stating that God is utterly and completely "set apart" from everything else in all of creation. There is no one and nothing like Him. This is a literal reality that is dependent upon His very nature and power, not our opinion!

To drive home the truth of this passage, underline the words *godlessness, unrighteousness, eternal power,* and *divine nature* in your Bible. Make a point during your conversation to note the vast differences between the defining characteristics of mankind and those of God. You may wish to mention other passages of Scripture, such as Isaiah six or Revelation four, to further establish the holiness of God. Also take a moment to remind your friend that according to what Scripture tells us here, no one has an excuse for denying the existence or holiness of God. He has revealed Himself through creation and even more so through His Son.

VERSE 2: MAN IS SINFUL

"All have sinned and fall short of the glory of God."Romans 3:23

Humans are as different from God as light is from darkness. As holy as God is, mankind is just as sinful and depraved. Some folks may take issue with this statement, but doing so places them in direct opposition to the claims of Scripture. The apostle Paul makes it clear that sin entered the world through Adam at the fall.[xl] In other words, at the moment that Adam chose to rebel against God's ownership and authority over his life, a sin nature sprung up within him that has since been a common thread in all humanity. This propensity for sin sets us violently against the holiness of God.

While Adam may have been the gateway through which this nature entered humanity, each individual bears sole responsibility for its presence and consequences in his own life. Some may attempt to argue that their sins are not as bad as those of others and are not as deserving of God's judgment. What must be remembered is that sin's burden has little to do with the severity of its consequences, but rather the rebelliousness it evidences against God in our lives.

You see, while we may argue that murder is worse than lying, both are affronts to the holy character and nature of God, the author of life and truth! Therefore, though the consequences of these two sins are very different, their severity is equal in the eyes of God. This revelation is precisely why Paul says that we are *all* guilty. Regardless of the size of our sin, the degree of our rebelliousness towards God is exactly the same.

What if someone doesn't know they've sinned? Are they still responsible before God? Some argue that it's unfair for God to hold people to a standard of which they know nothing about. Well, let me ask you a question. Let's say someone breaks into your home one night and beats you up, ties up your family, kills the family pet, and makes off with all of your valuables. Immediately you go through all the proper channels to report the crime, and thankfully days later the criminal is caught in the process of trying to sell your property. Now fast forward to the criminal's trial. As you sit in the court room hoping for justice, the judge asks the man, "How do you plea?" At this point, the criminal stands up and says, "Judge, I'm innocent. Yes, I broke into that house and did all those things, but I really didn't *know* it was wrong!" What would your response be? Would you suddenly be overwhelmed with pity for the man and beg that the charges be dropped? Would the realization that he didn't know that what he had done was wrong make his assault on your family and the sanctity of your home any less abhorrent to you? Would you stand up and demand that he be set free? I think not! Regardless of whether he knew that what he did was wrong or not, his behavior hurt you and your family. His ignorance doesn't erase the suffering he's caused you. More than just your property was stolen from you through his actions, and I'm pretty sure you'd demand justice, regardless of his proclaimed ignorance of the law.

There will be no one in all of creation who will be able to stand before the holy God of the universe and declare, "God, I just didn't know!" For one thing, based on what we've already talked about concerning His holiness, God has put a moral compass within each of us that convicts us all of wrong-doing. Recall that Romans 1:20 states that all people are without excuse before God. Not only that, but for God to regard one as sinless simply based on ignorance alone would make Him an unfair and unjust God, thus eradicating the holiness of His nature. Is wrong really any less wrong just because a perpetrator doesn't know it's wrong? Because of who He is, God must declare us all sinners regardless of our level of knowledge or spiritual insight.

One last point on this topic: I really don't think it's hard to perceive the inherent bent we all have towards sin. It really should come as no surprise to anyone that we are morally broken. If you ever have any doubt, just sit for a while and watch preschoolers play. While this age group hasn't really had the opportunity to be very much corrupted by society, they do a bang-up job of figuring out how to sin on their own! For those who would say that wrong-doing is a learned behavior, children muddy the water. The truth is that no one has to teach a child how to be self-centered, demanding, or short-tempered. The sin nature inside of them does all the training. There was a time in my life when I thought that kids came into the world as blank slates, later growing to be sinners. Then I had kids of my own! I can now attest to you with great confidence that children know how to sin way before anyone ever teaches them to do so…it's just in their nature!

So, we're left with two facts that create an eternally abysmal tension: God is completely holy while man is utterly sinful! No two differences could be more at odds with one another than these; nor could any have such eternal implications.

In order to make sure that your loved one doesn't miss the point of this passage, underline the words *all* and *sinned*. As you talk, elaborate on this concept, explaining that all sin is equally evil because it is an assault on the very character of God. Though the consequences may be more severe for some sins, the degree of evil is the same. While it is sometimes easy to justify one's goodness by pointing out the severity of others' sins, it's important to realize that from God's standpoint a "white lie" is just as evil as murder. This revelation means that all of us stand equally sinful before a holy God! There really is no such thing as a *good* person. This is a great opportunity for a bit of transparency as you admit that you struggle with sin just as much as the next person. In other words, you are no better than anyone else in any way!

VERSE 3: SIN BRINGS DEATH

"For the wages of sin is death…"Romans 6:23a

Isaac Newton's third law of motion states that there is an equal and opposite reaction for every action. If I drop a bowling ball from a skyscraper, the kinetic energy of the ball will ensure that some opposite reactions occur when it comes into contact with a sidewalk or an innocent passerby. This well known law, however, doesn't just apply to objects in motion. In every aspect of life, we understand that actions come with consequences. Generally speaking, good actions are followed by good consequences, while bad actions result in bad consequences.

This understanding takes us back, at least for a moment, to the presence and problem of evil in this world. I don't know if you've ever stopped to consider this or not, but we live in a broken world. Hate, envy, lust, greed, pollution, murder, theft, rape, abuse, you name it—all of these exist because of the evil bent that mankind has towards sin. Each of these things and a whole host more have their own set of consequences. The honest truth is that given any choice you and I are just as likely to choose wrong as right every single time! So, when one begins to think of the cumulative effects of all of our bad choices and the overlap between these, it's a real miracle that our world isn't in worse shape than it is.

Lets explore one example. A young man begins experimenting with alcohol as a teenager. After some time, he finds that he can't get away from the grip this drug has on his life. He has become an alcoholic. He battles with the effects of this addiction well into adulthood, leaving a broken family, damaged kids, and a ruined reputation in the fallout. Initially, his immediate family suffers the worst of the consequences as he is unable to hold down a job, supply their needs, or have genuine heart connections with those who need him most. Things progress, however, and one afternoon he decides to drive home after spending the evening feeding his intoxicating addiction, only to run through a red light and hit an oncoming school bus. The bus driver and many of the children are instantly killed. The resulting pain and suffering is immeasurable. Just for a moment, consider the far-reaching consequences from this one man's sins. The destruction of his own life and those of his family, the life-long struggles his behavior has produced in his own children, the lost lives and fractured families of those on the bus—one man's sin has wrought all manner of pain and suffering. One man's sin has produced consequences for a whole community! Now, multiply this by every sin that's ever been committed by every person who has ever lived on the face of this earth and you will join me in surprise not that God would allow evil to exist, but that He doesn't allow us to experience its full force!

You see, sin brings death! This death is both physical and spiritual. We physically die because of sin. The cumulative effects of our sin haven't just affected humanity, they've affected all of creation.

Through greed, negligence, competition, and lack of restraint, mankind has unleashed all manner of war, violence, chemicals, pollutants, abuses, and destruction on the earth. The effects of these things on our environment have resulted in sicknesses, disease, cancer, and death. No one can deny that mankind's actions have had an adverse effect on this world. Natural disasters occur as a result of a broken creation. Mechanical failures occur because someone somewhere cut a corner or tried to save a dime. Accidents happen because of human error, misjudgment, or lack of attention. While we may justify our deeds through what we consider good reasoning, we fail to take into account the unknown, cumulative burden our bad actions create in the world in which we live. Sin is the source of death, and we are the source of sin!

So, cumulatively and corporately the weight of sin in this world creates a never-ending cycle of pain, suffering, and death, but that's not all. Individually speaking, sin brings death. Despite the claims of Billy Joel back in the seventies that "only the good die young," it is quite obvious that a person's life expectancy is conversely proportionate to the degree of sin in his life. In other words, those who indulge in persistent sinful behavior generally live shorter lives. A promiscuous lifestyle puts one at a much higher risk of contracting a life-altering sexually transmitted disease. Heavy drug use destroys a body's systems and its ability to self-regulate. A violent lifestyle puts one at a considerably higher risk of dying a violent death. America suffers the stigma of being one of the most unhealthy and overweight nations in the world. Why? Because gluttony, licentiousness, and laziness have an affect on the body! The fact of the matter is that we spend a considerable amount of time and resources trying to minimize or avoid altogether the impending consequences of our bad behaviors. My sin will ultimately bring about my demise, and generally speaking the more I indulge my sinful nature, the more I hasten my impending doom.

Yes, the wages of sin really is death! I'm sure you've heard it said that "you've got to pay if you want to play." Regardless of what this statement originally meant, when it comes to sin this is oh so true. Many people never stop to consider the degree to which they are *playing* with sin or that there will be a day when the *payment* for all their playing will inevitably come. Wages are something you work for. You deserve them. They're owed to you! Truth be told, if you put in a good hard day's work and you don't get paid for it, you are pretty disappointed. Why then would we think God unfair when He allows us to spend our lives working to please our sin nature only to receive the payment that is due us…namely, death? You and I, because we all have sinned, deserve the death that is coming our way.

This death that we speak of isn't just physical, however. There is a spiritual aspect to it as well. God is the author, promoter, and source of life. In John 14:6, Jesus declares that He is "the way, the truth, and the life." In John 10:10, He says that His purpose in coming to earth is to provide people with abundant life. John 3:16 tells us that those who put their faith in Jesus will have eternal life. Jesus tells us in John 10:27-28 that His followers recognize His voice, follow Him, and that He gives them eternal life, the result of which is that they will "never perish!" Jesus described Himself as the "resurrection and the life" in John 11:25, going on to declare that those who believe in Him will never die. In John 12:50, Jesus describes the command of His Father as "eternal life." He instructs His disciples in Matthew 10:28 that they are not to fear those who may put them to death but that rather they should fear the one who is able to cast both body and soul into hell. So to be connected to God is to be connected to life, and to be separated from God is to be separated from life. This is a huge problem because, as we illustrated above, man's sinfulness is completely incompatible with God's holiness. In other words, we are disconnected from God. Like it or not, our default state is condemnation and spiritual death!

Matthew 25:46 is the culmination of Jesus' description of the Great Judgement. In this verse, Jesus declares that those who have faithfully served Him will enter into eternal life, while those who have not will be sent away to eternal punishment. We explored the reality of hell as we discussed 5 Reasons to Share a couple of chapters ago. As you think back over the Bible's description of hell, does it sound like a place of abundant or vibrant life? Absolutely not! God's Word is clear that just as sin brings about our physical death, it is also the cause of spiritual death. John 3:18 explains clearly that those who have no relationship with God exist in a default state of condemnation. They are, in essence, spiritually dead! And if they remain in that condition, all they have to look forward to is eternal death.

There is but one way to avoid death, and that is to choose Christ! Those of us who place our faith in Christ may taste physical death temporarily but will never experience true, eternal death! Not only that, we have the promise of God that physical death will not have the last word as we will be raised victorious! Unfortunately, many choose to reject Christ precisely because they feel that His teachings restrict their ability to live life to the fullest. What these people fail to realize is that by rejecting Him they are actually rejecting the only source of true life that is possible in all of eternity!

Every person who is born into this life begins dying the moment he is born. That's not morbid; it's truth! The fact is that all of us will die. There is no escaping the death awaiting each of us. Even secularists agree with us on this issue. Unless Christ returns before our day comes, each of us will feel the sting of death. While we may not like this, while we may spend our lives avoiding it, while we may try to convince ourselves otherwise, and while we may work daily to postpone the inevitable, there will come a day when we realize that the wages of sin truly is death! And whether we like it or not, death is exactly what we deserve.

Oh, how bleak an existence we would have if this were the end of the story! How hopeless we would be if death had the final say-so! It's a great weight, knowing your impending doom is coming with no real way to avoid it. No wonder so many people struggle with depression. No wonder people spend thousands of dollars each year on anything and everything that could add even one day to their lives. No wonder people try to get as much as they possibly can out of every day. You see, deep within each of us is a recognition that the reality of death applies to even us. We are all going to die! Furthermore, for those who die apart from Christ, physical death won't be the only death they will experience!

Thankfully, death doesn't have to have the final word! Jesus has defeated death! The wonderful and amazing truth is that though we all deserve death and hell, in abundant love God has made a way!

Underline the words *wages* and *death* in your Bible. It's important to fully explore the concept of wages. It will prove valuable for your loved ones to comprehend that death isn't just something that is doled out upon them. It's owed to them. This death, as we've noted, is both physical and spiritual. Emphatically point out that you realize that you deserve death yourself, explaining how the weight of such an understanding potentially leads to hopelessness. You may want to explain this by leading them to imagine that, apart from Christ, Satan is our employer, sin is our work, and death is our wage. Christ wants to destroy the power of Satan over our lives and set us free from all three.

VERSE 4: GOD HAS MADE A WAY!

"...but the gift of God is eternal life in Christ Jesus our Lord."Romans 6:23b

"While we were still helpless, at the appointed moment, Christ died for the ungodly. For rarely will someone die for a just person - though for a good person perhaps someone might even dare to die. But God proves His own love for us in that while we were still sinners Christ died for us."Romans 5:6-8

I love a good hero story. Anytime someone is willing to sacrifice to save another person, it's a story worth telling and retelling. In 1987 I was twelve years old. Twelve-year-olds don't usually pay much attention to world events, but to this day I remember the story surrounding a little girl named Jessica McClure. She was just eighteen months old when she fell twenty-two feet down a pipe leading to a well in her aunt's backyard in Midland, Texas. Immediately, rescuers sprang into action, working around the clock for over two days to save the little girl's life. I remember sitting glued to the television as we watched the story unfold before us. The entire nation was fixated on every detail. In fact, I'm pretty sure that a collective sigh of relief could be heard nationwide when the workers finally pulled Jessica from the depths of the ground. Make no mistake, there was no doubt in the minds of anyone watching that every single person who lent aid to Jessica and her family during that time was a hero!

I believe that the inherent emotional pull of this story sprang up in response to the helplessness of little Jessica. There was no way this small child had any chance of saving herself and no possibility of survival without outside assistance. There she was in the depths of the ground just waiting for someone, anyone, to lift her out. All things considered, I believe this story is a perfect analogy to our spiritual condition in relation to God!

You and I are helplessly entangled, caught in the depths of a struggle with sin for which we are completely ill-equipped. We are incapable of saving ourselves, and many of us are unable to even comprehend the true gravity of our plight! Sin has blinded us, mastered us, and threatens to ultimately destroy us. Death is all we have to look forward to as a reward for all of our playing with sin. Physical death will bring an end to all that we have lived to accomplish; and spiritual death promises to rob us of any hope of eternal happiness. No amount of good deeds can change this. No attempts to change the direction of our eternal destiny will be successful. Regardless of our efforts, we are hopelessly lost in sin. As rebellious enemies of a holy God, all we deserve is judgment and hell. We are helpless! However…and this is huge…rather than turn His back on humanity or demand that mankind pay the price for its rebellion, God demonstrated a love unlike any other by sending us a hero.

Imagine something with me for a moment. The rescue effort to save little Jessica McClure was supported fairly unanimously in our culture. After all, she was an innocent child. Consider how sentiment would have been different had we discovered that, instead of a small child, a serial killer in the act of stalking his next victim had fallen into a hole and become entrapped. To be sure, there still would have been some kind of rescue effort. However, I'm positive that there would be more than a few to claim that his predicament was the proper justice for his behavior. While workers would still have attempted to get him out, don't you know that their pace would in no way have approached the same fevered pitch as that of rescuing an innocent child. Take this a step further and ask yourself how you would respond had it been your loved one he was stalking and your well he fell into. You see, we are pretty swift to demand justice against those who have wronged us or even planned to do so!

Now, let's be clear about something. Just as you and I demand justice, so does God. He is a holy God, after all! To rebel against the God of the universe is no small thing. Restitution must be made! However, praise God that rather than requiring humanity to pay for its overindulgence in sin and selfishness, He chose to pour out His wrath on the only individual in all of existence who could suffer it and survive...Himself! You and I are the serial killer. Every day we find ourselves doing things that systematically destroy the image of God in us and the glory of God around us! Yet, instead of leaving us in the pit of sin, depravity, and death, God chose to join us there! He became a man, walked among those who profaned His name, lived with those corrupted by sin, ate with sinners, hung out with tax-collectors (who were mostly thieves) and prostitutes, endured the pains of a fallen creation, and then died in our place! That's right, God didn't just leave us in the pit, He joined us there. And then gave us the boost we needed to get out, taking our place alone!

What manner of love drives the judge to endure the punishment set aside for the criminal? How much must one care about another to willingly suffer at the hands of his enemies so that by his suffering the enemy may be saved? What drives the Creator to join in living alongside the created...experiencing hunger, sickness, betrayal, and death? What could possibly make Him willing to give up the justice owed to Him and offer instead unconditional forgiveness and complete repeal? I'll tell you that it's one thing and one thing alone: God's unmatched and unsurpassed love!

It's true that most of us would have a hard time giving up our lives for someone else. Perhaps, if it were a member of our family or someone we really cared about, we'd be willing to sacrifice ourselves for their good. We might possibly even consider making such a sacrifice if it involved some kind of lofty ideal which we were attempting to attain. If a person were worthy of living and if his life made the lives of others better, we might reason that our life was worth laying down in place of his. However, hardly anyone would be willing to trade his life for that of a hardened, murderous, conniving, unregenerate criminal. Yet that, my friends, is exactly what Christ did for us! Remember that our sin isn't just a matter of consequences. God doesn't hate our sin because of the problems it causes. He hates our sin because it is a personal attack on the very character and nature of His being. Our sin is a violent affront to who He is! The amazing truth of the gospel is that though we would set ourselves up as the vilest enemies of God, He still chooses to loves us and treat us as if we were His children!

Scripture makes His love for us quite clear even in light of our depraved condition. John explains how the creator of all things, the author of life, became a man, suffering rejection by many He came to save, yet offering adoption and life to all who would believe. This gospel book alone gives amazing details of why Jesus came and what He was up to:

- In one of the most famous passages in the Bible, Jesus teaches a Jewish leader by the name of Nicodemus that God's love for this world is so great that He is more than willing to sacrifice His own Son, Jesus, for the salvation of any who would trust Him (John 3:16).
- He taught the masses that just as bread and drink were important to the body's physical well-being, His body was offered for their spiritual survival (John 6:35-40).
- He explained that though mankind is a slave to sin, Christ came to set people free from slavery and to see them become children of God (John 8:34-36).
- While the consequences of sin is death, Jesus came in order to provide the opportunity for abundant and joyful life (John 10:10).
- Not only is this life abundant, it is eternal and irrevocable (John 10:27-30)!

- Now, there is no excuse for the lack of knowledge of who God is and how He loves us as, in His coming, Jesus fully revealed the Father and made a relationship with Him possible (John 12:44-50).
- In fact, Jesus alone is God's provision for salvation, making it possible to have a relationship with God and thus experience eternal life (John 14:6).
- Every bit of this work was accomplished as Jesus Christ suffered at the hands of sinners; He was betrayed by those closest to Him, wrongfully accused by His enemies, brutally mistreated and beaten at the hands of the Romans, and mercilessly hung on a cross to die, only to be raised victoriously three days later (John 18-20).

Why would Christ willingly leave His place in heaven, join us in our misery, and submit Himself to such suffering? Because of His love for you and me! Let's be clear about a few things here. Muhammed would strive to direct your paths and demand your obedience, but he would never die for you. Confucius would offer words of wisdom in hopes of leading you towards enlightenment, but he could never reveal God to you. Buddha might train you in the discovery of inner tranquility, but he could never free you from your bondage and slavery to sin. Joseph Smith and Charles Taze Russell would suggest ways to busy yourself with religious activity, but neither was capable of providing you with eternal life. Of all the leaders of world religions there is only one who has died for your sins, and on a side note, there is only one whose tomb now stands empty…that is Jesus Christ, the Messiah!

Jesus alone has made salvation, forgiveness, and eternal life possible! And get this: according to the second half of Romans 6:23, this life He offers is an unconditional gift. Rather than letting us have what we deserve—our "wages"—the Father offers us something completely unmerited, a gift of life through His Son Jesus. You see, for those who accept the gift, Jesus happily says, "Let me take the wage." Christ endured judgment, suffering, pain, and death on your behalf and mine. Only His life was enough to cover the debt created by our rebelliousness. It was only through His sacrifice that we could be forgiven. He who was sinless was made to be sin for us so that we might become righteous before God.[xli] "He was delivered up for our trespasses and raised for our justification."[xlii] God's immeasurable love was demonstrated in sending His one and only Son into the world that we may live through Him. "Love consists in this: not that we loved God, but that He loved us and sent His Son to be a propitiation for our sins."[xliii] Rejoice because God has truly made a way in Jesus. He is "the way, the truth, and the life!"

In the latter part of Romans 6:23, underline the words *gift* and *eternal life*. Discuss the difference between a wage and a gift. Obviously, a wage is something that is owed to you, while a gift is something that is graciously given. Explain that the gift of God is just like any other gift. Though it is offered, it does not become yours until you accept it! Gifts are never forced on others! In Romans 5:8, underline the words *love*, *sinners*, and *died*. Ask your friend to explain, based on this verse, how God went about making this gift of grace available. Make sure he understands that Christ died in order for this to be possible. Explain that Scripture makes it clear that Christ lived a completely sinless life. That means that since death is the wage of sin, He must have died for someone's sin other than His own. To drive this idea home a bit more, you may wish to explore the last few chapters of any of the gospels to provide a clear narrative of the death, resurrection, and ascension of Christ. Hopefully, your friend will begin to see the extent to which God went to demonstrate His love for us through the cross.

VERSE 5: TRUST AND OBEY

> *"This is the message of faith that we proclaim: if you
> confess with your mouth, 'Jesus is Lord,' and believe in
> your heart that God raised Him from the dead, you
> will be saved. With the heart one believes, resulting in
> righteousness, and with the mouth one confesses, resulting
> in salvation....Everyone who calls on the name of the
> Lord will be saved."Romans 10:9-10, 13*

The concept of lordship has largely been lost in modern day American culture. We are taught from a young age that we have the power to control our own destinies, and we pride ourselves in being self-made people. The *American Dream* compels each of us not to live in subjection to another person, but to become masters over our own little kingdoms. These kingdoms all look a little different. Some set out to build an empire by way of business. Others seek to build a family or a home. For a few, their kingdoms are based upon the fulfillment of childhood dreams. These dream-chasers sacrifice much in other areas of their lives to see their desires fulfilled. Regardless of what these kingdoms look like, the "masters" or "lords" at the center of each are all the same: us!

In America, the greatest hurdle to one's coming to Christ is not a despotic government or an oppressive dominant religion, but an individual's refusal to give up ownership and mastery of his own life in order to submit to God. When Paul says that a key component to true salvation is an acknowledgment that Christ is one's Lord, he's making a statement that flies in the face of the fierce individualism that marks our day.

To fully understand what lordship entails, let us think back to the days of lords and servants. According to Webster's Dictionary, a *lord* is "a ruler by hereditary right or preeminence to whom service and obedience are due."[xliv] Lords held supreme power over all their subjects. Loyal obedience was expected, and disobedience carried stiff consequences. A subject's refusal to surrender allegiance was seen as the highest form of treason. This is precisely the understanding Paul's original hearers had of the concept of lordship. So, when Paul says we are to confess Christ as Lord, he is unapologetically stating that we must acknowledge Christ's authority over all things in the universe, including ourselves. Remember that Jesus Himself claimed this authority after the resurrection as He proclaimed to the disciples that all authority in heaven and earth had been given to Him.[xlv]

John's gospel acknowledges the supreme authority of Christ in its opening sentences, stating that Christ, being completely God, existed from eternity, exercising the very power and authority of God in the creation of all that is. Just as there is no doubt of God's holiness or power, there is no denying that Christ reigns supreme as Lord! This is a fact that remains true regardless of mankind's opinion on the matter. In fact, Scripture claims that though some may refuse to willingly accept His lordship over them now, there will come a day when at the name of Jesus every knee will bow and every tongue confess that He is Lord.[xlvi] The mark of a true believer is that his faith in Christ drives him to let go of his own kingdom, eschew his own will, and joyfully proclaim Christ as Lord now!

Of course, to proclaim Christ as Lord is more than just a cliche´ or a statement of consent. Rather, it is the inauguration of a lifestyle of service and submission to His teachings and commands. The person who truly makes Christ lord gives up ownership of his life, accepting the role of servant, disciple, and ambassador for Christ's kingdom. While these individuals continue to exist in this world, conducting their businesses and living their lives, each decision they make is done so at the consent of the Savior. To make Christ one's Lord entails a radical reorienting of one's life around His words and His ways. It involves a transfer of ownership as we give up the reigns of our lives, trusting Jesus' leadership and direction over our own. To acknowledge His lordship is to join Him in what He says is important, willingly leaving behind those things for which we previously strived.

A servant follows his master, learning from him and joining him in what he does. Such is the case for all who claim Christ as Lord! Those of us who follow Him willingly abandon efforts to build our own kingdoms in the passionate pursuit of investing our lives in His. Living for one's self is no longer appealing as believers have been offered a higher calling in living for Jesus, pointing others to His goodness. Indulging in sinful pleasure is forsaken for the joy that comes from faithfully serving the one who sacrificed Himself that we might have life. All of this is to say that confessing Christ as Lord is as much a matter of the heart and will as it is a matter of the mind!

An important point that must be enforced is that there is no way to divorce true, saving faith in Christ from submission to the lordship of Christ. For decades, Christian pastors have encouraged people to walk down aisles, proclaiming faith in the death, burial, and resurrection of Jesus. Once this occurs, the process of discipleship often begins with a focus on training people to come under the leadership and lordship of Jesus. While I wholeheartedly endorse efforts to bring people to Christ, I believe that we have often gotten the cart before the horse. Scripture makes it clear, directly as well as narratively, that one does not come to Christ as Savior without also coming to Him as Lord. In fact, it can be argued that acknowledging Jesus' authority over our lives as well as this world is the first step in coming to a true, saving faith! To think that we may attain the blessings of the cross without the burden of denying ourselves and taking up the cross[xlvii] is to, in essence, make us the master and Jesus the servant. Such a decision demonstrates a rebellious and unrepentant heart. In other words, you may have Jesus as your *Lord* and Savior or you may not have Him at all.

If acknowledging Christ as Lord provides a basis for faith, exercising belief in His work on the cross demonstrates the substance of faith. One benefit of living in a postmodern, technology driven society is the availability of endless volumes of information that are accessible at the press of a button. This luxury, however, has led to a basic misunderstanding of what it means to actually "believe." It is quite possible for me to find an abundance of information on George Washington or the Taj Mahal. Though I may know many facts about each, however, I have never personally met George Washington or visited the Taj Mahal. I can accept all of the facts about each, convincing myself that I do indeed believe in these things without any amount of experience to back up my belief. You see, it is experience that moves us past cognitive assent to emotional investment. I also know many facts about my family. Yet, what I believe about them carries a different degree of authenticity and sincerity for me because this belief carries with it an emotional investment. My future is tied to theirs. My well-being is, in many ways, dependent upon theirs. The things I know to be true of them are not based on facts someone has shared with me, but on experiences that I have personally witnessed and am willing to stake my life upon. While I might fight, suffer, or die for what I believe about my family, I would never do so for those things which are simply intellectual facts. Press me and I'll change my beliefs about George Washington, but no amount of pressure could change my beliefs about those whom I love. Such is the essence of true belief in Christ!

Truthfully, this is where some folks' Christianity falls short. There are those who accept facts about Jesus' redemptive work as truth. Cognitively, they really do believe that there was a historical figure named Jesus who died on a cross and rose from the grave. Yet, their level of investment as a result of that belief is minimal. Because they have not given their lives to Christ, they are not emotionally or willfully invested in a relationship with Him. This is precisely why I say that acknowledgement of Christ's lordship is the basis for faith. When you and I are ready to accept the claims of Christ as real and applicable to us as individuals, then we are ready to exercise a faith that goes deeper than accepting a set of facts. To believe in one's heart is to be willing to stake one's very life on the truth that is claimed! It is to hold so firmly to what you know in your heart to be true that there is nothing or no one who could change your mind. This type of belief involves an emotional and volitional investment. Because I believe so passionately, I am willing to risk everything. And the fact that I'm willing to risk everything creates an emotional investment that only drives me deeper in my belief.

Think about this for a moment: if Christ really did die for our sins and rise from the dead, then that moment in history has changed everything! Conversely, if He didn't rise from the dead, then believers are fools. As Paul stated, if the hope of Christ is for this life alone, believers are to be pitied above anyone else![xlviii] The point is that "weak belief" actually makes no sense. Either Jesus is who Scripture claims He is *and* He demands and deserves your very life and soul, or He's not, and we are fools to hold on to any false pretenses that He is anything more than an interesting historical figure. Paul would emphatically state that Christ has been raised from the dead, that Scripture is accurate in all it says about Him, and that we would do well to give ourselves to Him in joyful submission. I accept this as a remarkable testimony for one reason…Paul was willing to die for this belief! And not only Paul! Every single disciple, except John, died precisely because of his faith in Christ. Even John suffered, spending his last years in exile. Every single New Testament writer experienced persecution after persecution because of belief in Jesus as Savior. The sincerity of their faith is a testament to the reality of the cross and the empty tomb. Not only this, I have personally experienced Christ in my own life! I am emotionally invested in Him, and He is invested in me! Because I trust Him, I obey Him; and because I obey Him, I am driven to trust Him even more!

This, my friend, is what is required in order for salvation to take place in anyone's life…to trust and obey! To be sure, salvation is a gift that you and I did absolutely nothing to make possible. By the love of the Father, this gift is freely made available. However, hold no false hope that taking hold of this gift will cost you nothing because the opposite is actually true! It will cost you everything. In fact, it will cost you your very being! The transaction of salvation is a miraculous event whereby we give up ownership of our lives and receive *real* life in return! Sounds a lot like something Jesus said doesn't it? "The one who loves his life will lose it, and the one who hates his life in this world will keep it for eternal life."[xlix]

As you lead your friend to explore this passage, underline the words *confess*, *Lord*, *believe*, and *saved*. Fully explain what it means to confess Christ as Lord. Make sure that your friend understands that Christ demands that we come to Him on His terms, which always means unconditional surrender. Discuss the concept of lordship. I'm sure that if someone were to walk in on one of my conversations, at this point, it would probably sound like I'm trying to talk someone out of following Jesus. The truth is that I don't want people going into this decision blind. Folks need to know what they are committing themselves to. Spend time talking about the difference between accepting facts—something we often refer to as belief—and true belief which bears itself out in a willingness to stake one's entire future on the truth one claims. Another example that I often use is the difference between accepting that an airplane will fly and actually flying on the plane. The first is simply agreeing to a scientific theory or truth, while the latter requires one to invest his very life in that belief. This second type of belief is what is required of those who would come to Jesus.

CONCLUSION

At this point, you have clearly made the truth of the gospel available to your friend. As God has spoken through His word, you can rest assured His Holy Spirit has been at work. Now would be the perfect time to ask your friend or loved one if there has ever been a time in his life when he acknowledged Christ as Lord and exercised faith in His death, burial, and resurrection. If he says he's never done so, invite him to do it immediately.

Let's be very clear about one thing here. If someone has made Christ Lord and Savior, he will know it. If he is unsure, you must treat that response just as if he has answered "no." To say that following Christ is a life and death decision is actually to put it too lightly. We are talking about eternity here, so there is no room for uncertainty. If the one you are sharing with is uncertain, encourage him to act on faith now to ensure certainty!

If you have been praying for your friend ahead of time and have continued to pray throughout your conversations then you can rest assured that God has been at work. Whether the other responds in faith or not, you can confidently know two things. First, you have been faithful to do what Christ has called you to do in sharing your faith. Second, God will continue to work in the life of your loved one.

In the next chapter, we will look at possible responses to what has been shared here. Of course, the answer you are hoping and praying for is that the other person is ready and willing to call on Christ in faith. If he is prepared to do so, you will find good information on how to lead him to respond as you continue reading. What if, however, he gives some other response? In the next chapter, I will share with you 5 Possible Responses you may expect from folks with whom you share.

There is something I would like to address before we move on. If your friend responds in any way other than with faith, you might feel discouraged, especially if you've spent weeks or months building to this point. Let me encourage you with a few thoughts. First, remember that God has said His Word does not return to Him void but accomplishes all that He sends it to do. The reason you had your friend go straight to Scripture rather than sharing your own words, was to create the opportunity for him to intimately interact with God's Word. Trust that His Word is at work. We have the promise that God's Word is "living and effective and sharper than any two-edged sword, penetrating as far as to divide soul, spirit, joints, and marrow; it is a judge of the ideas and thoughts of the heart."[l] Though your friend may seem to reject Christ off the cuff, days later God's Word may still be penetrating the depths of his heart, driving him towards repentance. Don't lose hope; continue to pray! Secondly, rest assured that God loves and cares for your friend more than you possibly ever could. In fact, Scripture makes it clear that His will is for all to find life in His Son.[li] Finally, be at peace, knowing that you have been obedient to live a powerful witness in front of your loved one. Continue to display a consistent testimony, praying that others may see your example and come to glorify God themselves.[lii]

5

Possible Responses

God's Word is powerful. This is a truth we discussed in depth in the last chapter. An inherent quality of His Word is that it demands a response. It is utterly impossible to hear from God and not make some kind of a decision. One will either acknowledge the authority of His Word and act in complete surrender, or one will deny its power and live in disobedience. The one thing that no one will do, however, is remain neutral to its claims. There is no room for riding the fence when it comes to the Bible.

In his book *Knowing God,* J. I. Packer states, "God sends His Word to us in the character of both information and invitation. It comes to woo us as well as to instruct us; it not merely puts us in the picture of what God has done and is doing, but also calls us into personal communion with the loving Lord Himself."[liii] God's Word is an invitation to join Him. As with any invitation, a response is required.

When I receive an invitation to some activity, there are really only two ways I can respond. I either accept and begin making plans to attend or reject the invitation. You may assume that there is another option. Perhaps I could just ignore the invitation altogether, as if it was never received. However, to ignore the invitation has the same outcome as rejecting it. In essence, to avoid making a decision is a decision not to accept.

So, there are basically two ways that people will respond to the gospel as it's been presented. They may accept its truth and joyfully surrender themselves to Jesus or reject its claims and refuse its blessings for their lives. This rejection may be demonstrated in different ways. Your friend may object to periphery issues that have nothing to do with the gospel. This is precisely the tactic that the woman at the well used when Jesus pressed her concerning her sinful lifestyle.[liv] One may understand quite well the demands of Scripture, but not be ready to surrender. This is actually a much more honest answer than others. Perhaps, one will fall back on a faulty understanding of salvation or seek to mix what he's just been exposed to with some other belief system to make it more palatable. Whatever the case, make no mistake that the only proper response to a presentation of the gospel is immediate surrender.

In this chapter, we will explore five possible responses to the gospel message as explained in the last chapter. Of course, all but one of these would be considered a "no" response to the gospel. Hopefully, by preparing for the possibility of hearing one or more of these responses, you can begin to think through how you might have a conversation concerning each. Remember that just as in every other area of this approach spiritual conversations are part of the goal. Just because your friend rejects the gospel message now doesn't mean he will continue to do so. How you react to him will lay the foundation for on-going conversations in the future. Remember that you do not ever want to become confrontational or burn any bridges.

The goal is to continue to have spiritual conversations with this person. Regardless of the direction these conversations take, you can continue to pray for him and look for opportunities in the future.

RESPONSE 1: I WANT TO KNOW JESUS

It goes without saying that this is the response we hope for when we share the gospel with someone. If your friend shares that he is ready to begin a relationship with Jesus it means that every investment you've made is about to pay off! It's quite acceptable to be excited and to show that you are!

As you've explained the gospel, God has been revealing Himself through Scripture. His Holy Spirit has been working to open the eyes of your loved one to his need for Him. He has been quickening understanding of all that Christ did on the cross to pay the wages of sin and offer him the gift of eternal life. At this point, the ball is squarely in your friend's court. However, he may be unsure of how to proceed. This is where some facilitation on your part comes in. You will have the wonderful privilege of taking your friend by the hand and leading him into an eternal relationship with the author of life and liberty.

Obviously, a faith response to Christ involves much more than just a simple prayer. After all, we are talking about a life transformation. It has been said that a "journey of one thousand miles begins with one step." The same is true of an eternal relationship with Jesus. That first step is a simple prayer. Responding to Christ's invitation through prayer is the practical beginning point of any relationship with Him.

At this juncture, let me encourage you to remind your loved one of a couple of things. First, prayer is not magic! When we pray to God,

His response is not based on our using just the right words or the passion with which we speak. God knows and perceives the motives of our hearts. He sees and understands the passion behind each prayer. While prayer may be an outward expression of inner feelings, it is nothing more than a simple tool for communication. It is what is going on inside one's heart that really matters to God. Second, remember that we are inviting people to enter into a relationship, not a contract! Just because someone admits, believes, and confesses doesn't mean they are saved. It is quite possible to do each as a matter of works, not as a personal response to join Christ in an intimate relationship. We are not encouraging our friends to be more religious, but to go deep in relationship!

I know that most of us have experienced being led to pray, or perhaps we've even led others to pray a "repeat after me" prayer. I would advise against this method. When a person reaches out to Christ, he needs to realize that he isn't reliant on any other person in doing so. Just as Christ alone was enough to pull sinking Peter from the stormy waves, so He alone is capable of drawing one who calls on His name out of the depths of sin. One potential pitfall of a "repeat" prayer is that it creates a level of dependency right out of the gate for spiritual growth. You will encourage folks to continue praying to God after this initial prayer, but what if they don't have someone to tell them what to pray the next time they go to God? A better approach would be to explain the proper attitude and response that must be part of this initial prayer, then set the person free to pray as his own heart directs him. Another danger of having someone repeat my words is that they are *my* words! Remember that though we all come to the Father through the same door, we all get to that door in a little bit different way. Each of us has an individual and unique relationship with Christ. I believe that the way each relationship begins should be just as unique…especially in what we say to Him. It's much better to teach someone to pour his heart out to Christ and trust that He will meet him where he is rather than to involve him in a cookie-cutter prayer experience.

How does one go about identifying the proper way to call on Christ for salvation? Thankfully, the Bible has already answered that question. In fact, you've already shared the answer. Remind your friend that according to Romans 10:9-10 the only way to experience the gift of salvation is by trusting and obeying Christ. To be more specific, this passage tells us that we must express sincere faith in the death, burial, and resurrection of Christ and declare our unconditional surrender to Him as Lord. Both of these prerequisites must be met in order for true salvation to take place. As already stated, the kind of belief that is required goes further than just a mental assent. The fact that we are willing to surrender our entire lives proves our belief out. Regardless of the words used, your loved one must communicate to the Father that he is ready to give over complete control of His heart and life to Christ based on his belief that Christ's death was a sacrificial atonement made on his behalf.

Remember that it's the attitude of the heart that counts here! If your loved one doesn't get in all of the traditional "ABCs," don't sweat it as long as you know he is voicing real faith through surrender. I have made the mistake in the past of believing that a lost person could not do this on his own. I felt as though I needed to give him the exact words to say, and if he didn't say those words exactly right, we needed to go through the whole process again. Over the years God convicted me that He can see my friend's heart, though all I hear are his words. You see, it is quite possible for someone to perfectly repeat my words without actually engaging in a true act of faith from the heart. Obviously, this behavior would not result in salvation even though I might feel confident of my friend's decision based on what I saw and heard. On the other hand, someone may completely make a shipwreck out of the prayer I instruct him to recite, but still make a genuine heart connection with God. This revelation led me to stop using the "repeat after me" prayer. Now I spend time talking about what must happen in the heart and then set the person free to express that in his own words. I can tell you that this change in approach has allowed me to be witness to some amazingly genuine, heart-felt conversations with God. It is obvious when someone opens his heart to the Father. I've never been brought to tears while telling someone what to pray, but I have been overcome with emotion listening to people I care about pouring their hearts out before God. All of this is to say that we must remember that our job is to facilitate conversation between our friends and God, not to force it.

Follow up this prayer by encouraging your friend with the words of Romans 10:13, "Everyone who calls on the name of the Lord will be saved." Assure him that if he was honest in his surrender to Christ and the expression of his faith, he can rest assured that Christ has saved him! By the way, you should also express your excitement and happiness over his decision!

Having called on the name of Jesus in faith, it's time to encourage him to take some next steps of faith. First of all, explain the importance of studying God's Word. Paul made it very clear that the Bible is a powerful and excellent source of instruction when it comes to spiritual life saying, "All Scripture is inspired by God, and is profitable for teaching, for rebuking, for correcting, for training in righteousness, so that the man of God may be complete, equipped for every good work."[lv] A good place to encourage a friend to start in Bible study is the Gospel of John. This Gospel is easy to read and illustrates very clearly the depths of God's love for this world. Suggest that he follow this up by studying John's first letter.

In addition to Bible study, church attendance is a must for a growing believer. No Christian was meant to exist as an island. In fact, when believers separate themselves from other Christ-followers, they are setting themselves up for some pretty serious moral failures. The church provides a place of belonging and fellowship. Believers are a source of encouragement as well, pushing one another towards greater spiritual maturity and providing strength in times of weakness or need. Paul taught the church at Corinth that the church is like a body. Each member serves an important role, and anyone's absence hampers the work of the overall body. Of course, being part of the body will also mean taking part in the ordinances that Christ Himself established...baptism and communion.

Every new believer needs to realize from the start that followers of Christ go where He is and do what He does. In other words, find out what Christ is doing around you and get involved. One way this will be fleshed out is in leading others to Jesus. In Matthew 13 Jesus shares the Parable of the Sower, explaining that those with a true saving faith *always* produce fruit. In other words, true believers reproduce themselves by leading others to be believers. The concept of a person living twenty or so years as a Christian without leading anyone to Christ is no where to be found in the Bible—at least not in a favorable light. True disciples make disciples! Honestly, I wish someone had told me this as a new Christian. It would have saved me many years of fruitless living.

One last thing...just because your friend has made a decision to follow Christ doesn't mean that you are now off the hook. New Christians are like children. There are some things they can do spiritually speaking for themselves, but there are a vast number of things they need to learn. Your job now shifts from having spiritual conversations in hopes of leading your friend to Christ to having conversations in hopes of helping him to grow in Christ. You must take on the role of teacher as you continue to demonstrate to your loved one what it looks like to be a Christ-follower. Hold him accountable, share what God is doing in your life, and watch in amazement as Christ works in and through the life of your friend.

RESPONSE 2: I'll DO IT LATER

People are great at putting off until later what needs to be done today. This fact isn't just true of work, but also of important decisions. In fact, the larger and more impactful the decision to be made, the more likely we are to want to put it off to the very last minute.

The problem with this behavior, especially when it comes to deciding on a relationship with Christ, is that being human means never knowing when your time is going to run out. I recently watched a video of an avalanche that occurred on Mt. Everest. The video was taken in a base camp directly in the path of the oncoming avalanche. The videographer lived through the ordeal, taking refuge inside a tent. However, the part of the video that held me in utter amazement was what the person was doing as he was trying to scramble to safety. He wasn't praying, nor was he calling out to God. Instead, he was repeating an expletive over and over again, almost as if it were a mantra. I'm pretty sure he didn't realize he was even saying this as the obvious priority on his mind was getting to safety so that his life might be preserved.

The actions of this videographer drive home why putting off a decision for Christ is so dangerous. Many people live their lives as if they will never die or, at least, that they will not die anytime soon. The Hollywood death scenes we see in movies have led many to believe that there will be plenty of time at the end to say those last words and get our affairs in order for eternity. However, the truth is that people die every day, and many of them have death overtake them at the least expected moment. Few people are actually ready to die when the time comes! The fellow in the avalanche video was so invested in trying to save his life that I'm sure he gave no thought to what would happen to him in the next few moments if his actions were unsuccessful! This is a truth that must be explained if your friend states that he'll make a decision for Christ at a more convenient time. None of us is promised another minute on this earth, and to put off a decision that so heavily determines our eternity is the utmost in recklessness.

Let's be honest. Usually the reason people want to put off this decision is because they know a relationship with Christ will significantly alter the course of their lives and they just aren't ready to give over the reins to someone else. When a person says this to you, it should immediately be flagged as an issue with Christ's lordship. Quite often folks realize their need for the Savior, but are unwilling to relinquish control of their lives to Christ. In putting off a decision, they hope to be able to continue to live their lives on their terms and give themselves to Christ at the last possible minute. To be sure, most imagine that this will be when they're old and gray and have spent the majority of their lives pursuing their own hopes and dreams. If by some bad stroke of luck their time is up sooner rather than later, they anticipate that they will have enough time in the moments before they die to cry out to Jesus. It doesn't take a genius to see the eternal danger inherent in such a decision.

Jesus told a story about a man who was more interested in his current life than the eternal. According to Jesus, there was a rich man whose land produced an overabundance of goods. This being the case, virtually overnight the man became very wealthy. His response to this situation was to tear down his old barns and build bigger ones to store up all his wealth. After having done this, he planned to sit back, relax, and enjoy life. "But God said to him, 'You fool! This very night your life is demanded of you. And the things you've prepared—whose will they be?' That's how it is with the one who stores up treasure for himself and is not rich toward God."[lvi] This rich man thought he had plenty of life left to live. I'm sure he thought he'd have plenty of time to get prepared for eternity.

Another story that Jesus shared involved a rich man and a fellow named Lazarus. Lazarus was a beggar who loved God, and when death ultimately found him, he ended up in paradise. The rich man, however, had no time for God and spent his days in selfish and lavish living. When death unexpectedly found him, he ended up in hell. There in torment he begged that someone might go to his brothers to warn them of the fate that awaited them if they did not turn to God in repentance. However, the clear answer was that they had all the invitation to eternal life that they would ever get. If they continued to reject God, their fate would be sealed as well.[lvii] It mattered not that this man had all the luxuries of life, for he quickly realized that the torments of eternity would make his time on earth seem like nothing more than a breath.

Many people who have been prayed for over the years continue to live under the self-delusion that they have all the time in the world to get right with God. They have felt God draw them, had their eyes open to their need for Christ, had Christians reach out to them, they may have even had events happen in their lives that really drew their attention towards God; yet in the face of God's offer of grace, they choose to remain neutral. In their minds, they're not saying "no" to God; they're simply saying "not right now." The hard cold facts, however, are that any decision other than unconditional surrender of one's life is a rejection of what Christ offers.

Revelation 3:20 is a perfect example of the condition of these folks' hearts. In this passage, Jesus declares, "Listen! I stand at the door and knock. If anyone hears My voice and opens the door, I will come in to him and have dinner with him, and he with Me." Jesus is constantly knocking at the doors of the hearts of people who respond, "Come back another time, Jesus. I'm just not ready." The sad fact is that there is a great possibility that the circumstances of their lives may so busily entangle them that they may never find time to open the door. Or perhaps rejection after rejection leads to the day when the knocking at the door stops altogether!

If this is your friend's response, your first question should be "Why?" Why would a person be willing to gamble with his eternity? What could possibly be so great in this life that he would risk sacrificing eternity to have it? How could one know the sacrifice made by Christ in order to make grace available to him and not immediately seize it? What could this world possibly offer that remotely compares with the promise of eternal life? As you talk about this, make your friend clearly and distinctly put into words why he believes that another time would be better to surrender to Christ. Make sure he understands the claims of the gospel and all that was revealed in the verses you've discussed. Use the material here to help him understand that time is limited and that death often overtakes us when least expected.

Encourage your loved one that it is never wise to put off Christ when He calls you. See how Paul exhorted the Corinthians. "Don't receive God's grace in vain. For He says, 'In an acceptable time, I heard you, and in the day of salvation, I helped you.' Look, now is the acceptable time; look, now is the day of salvation."[lviii] The writer of Hebrews puts it this way, "Today, if you hear His voice, do not harden your hearts as in the rebellion….Therefore, while the promise remains of entering His rest, let us fear so that none of you should miss it."[lix] Scripture clearly teaches that by putting off a decision to follow Christ, many will miss out on eternal life!

While this may be a passionate topic for you to discuss, I would again remind you to leave the door open to further conversation. If your loved one remains resistant to making a decision, pray fervently over the days and weeks to come that God would convince him of his need to take Christ up on His offer of grace. Pray that he gets no rest and that God would constantly remind him of the brevity of life until he is willing to forsake all to follow Christ. Look for opportunities to continue your conversation. Live a life in front of them that clearly demonstrates the joy and peace that comes from complete surrender to Christ. Help him to understand that Christ's burden is indeed light and His yoke is easy.[ix] Let him see Christ's peace reigning in you as you live a life of obedience and love before him.

REASON 3: CHRISTIANS ARE HYPOCRITES

As believers, we place a lot of emphasis on having a good reputation. However, as valuable as a good standing before others is, I believe that true character is much more important. What's the difference? Well, reputation is what people put on your tombstone while character is what angels whisper about you in the courts of heaven. Reputation encompasses who people think you are; character is the real you. Character is who you are when no one is looking and there is no one but God to impress. Christians focus a lot on reputation, but I think we should focus more on character. I believe I'm not the only one who thinks this way.

We live in a world that is constantly watching believers to see if they really are all that they claim to be. An observing world wants to know if a relationship with Jesus will really change a person. Many claim that Christian belief is just a crutch used by folks who are weak minded or emotionally fragile. Unfortunately, believers unintentionally feed this mentality when they live lives that are inconsistent with the teachings of Christ. In recent years there have been numerous cases of highly respected Christian leaders whose moral failures have caused unbelievers to question the character of all Christians. It is quite obvious that weaknesses in our testimonies reflect poorly on the power of God's Spirit in us. It seems that we live in a society where some new scandal involving a follower of Jesus headlines the news on an all too regular basis. This does little to engender trust in the hearts and minds of a lost world.

As I've shared my faith with people over the years, I've run into some who admit that they would come to Jesus but for one thing: they actually know some "Christians." Invariably, these people would tell me, "Well, you see the problem is that I know some people you go to church with and let me tell you they're a bunch of hypocrites!" What do you think my response is to these kinds of accusations? You might be surprised to find out that I don't disagree with them! I know that there are hypocrites in the church. The truth is that all believers are hypocrites to a small degree as the standard Jesus lays out for us is perfection and none of us meet that standard this side of heaven. However, I know the critics aren't talking about this sort of hypocrisy. The world realizes we're not perfect, and quite honestly, they don't expect us to be. However, they do expect that we would be different in some measurable way from those who don't claim faith at all. When they speak of hypocrisy, they refer to folks who claim to believe in Jesus but demonstrate no evidence of faith. Even more so, they specifically point out those who hold others to a higher standard than they hold themselves. Both become major stumbling blocks to unbelievers.

I remember a conversation I had with a young man a few years back. He was sitting a couple of machines over from me in the gym where I was working out. Hearing the music coming from his headphones, I was immediately interested. He was listening to a crossover band that hovered on the line between secular and Christian. Recognizing an opportunity, I struck up a conversation with him about the particular song he was listening to. As we talked, I discovered that he was actually a believer. Surprisingly, however, he revealed that he didn't go to church anywhere. When I pushed him a little on that issue, he explained that he had tried numerous churches in the area. The problem was that he was covered in tattoos, had numerous piercings, and dressed with a definite rockstar flair. He explained that when he walked into a sanctuary, everyone's head turned as if on swivels. Evidently, some well-meaning folks at one church even told him that if he wanted to come back, he needed to dress a little better for the occasion. These were supposed to be people who demonstrated the love of Christ, yet all he felt was condemnation and judgment over the way he looked. He perceived hypocrisy, and that was enough to turn him away. He made it clear to me that though he loved Jesus, he couldn't be around God's people. The sad thing was that I was afraid to invite him to my church for fear that the same thing might happen to him there.

Whenever someone points out hypocrisy in the church, I just can't disagree with them. In fact, they're usually surprised by how much I do agree with them! Hypocrisy frustrates me just as much as it does them, possibly even more! After being in ministry for over twenty years, I can honestly say that the things that turn me off to church life the most often involve some of the people in the church! Some folks just don't seem to be the real deal. This doesn't mean you and I aren't called to love these people. We must love them because Christ does. However, let's be realistic about the fact that hypocrisy exists in a major way in today's church culture.

We all like to be able to trust people. When we come across someone who claims to be one kind of person, yet whose actions prove them to be something else, the encounter makes us leery and more than a little uncomfortable. So if you run into this response, don't even try to argue the point. Admitting that some folks who call themselves Christians fall pretty far short of the mark will take the wind out an antagonist's sails pretty quickly.

Arguing the point is useless. The proper response would be to remind your friend that you're not asking him to follow Christians. You're inviting him to follow Jesus! And here's the deal: Jesus has never been untruthful! No dishonesty has ever been found in Him. Since before the dawn of creation, He has been ever true to His character and nature. He not only was the same in public and private, He is the same yesterday, today, and forever![lxi] He will never let your friend down and he can always look to Him for the perfect example of how to live a life filled with peace, joy, happiness, and holiness.

I know that sometimes it's the very leaders of the church who seem to cause the most damage in this area. I would point out that a church leader who isn't following Christ really isn't a leader at all. In my mind, leadership is really all about following. My job as a minister is to follow Christ so that, as they follow me, others can always look past me to see Jesus. I've made it pretty clear during all my years of ministry that I don't want any of my students to look to me as their model for Christ-likeness. I realize that at some point regardless of how hard I try I may let them down. Since I don't want their faith to be crushed by my failures, I refer them straight to Jesus. If they will look to Him, they'll never be disappointed! My hopes and prayers are that as they look at Him, they will be able to look past me. I must admit that there have been times when they've actually stepped ahead of me—when I've been challenged by their passion and commitment. In those times, I've had to hustle to get back to my proper position in the line-up. However, make no mistake; though I may be a few steps ahead of them, I am not the leader…Christ is!

As you discuss this issue, try not to get too deep into specific instances of hypocrisy. At the same time, be cognizant of the fact that you may have a friend who has been deeply hurt by Christians at some point in his life. It may be true that the only way he'll ever be able to move past this stumbling block is to have you listen, validate his feelings, and remind him that though Christians are God's people, they are not God! Gently remind him that there is no reason that *he* should miss out on the gift of grace simply because others abuse it.

If after talking about this response, your friend is ready to turn his life over to Jesus, rejoice and lead him to do so. Otherwise, agree to talk again about the issue later. Perhaps, as he watches you live out your faith in authenticity, he'll be drawn to the understanding that Christ really does make a difference in the lives of true believers. Pray that he'll be able to see through his own cynicism to his personal need for Christ and what He wants to do for him. When opportunities arise, bring up examples of people living out their faith in conversation. Above all, continue to trust God to work in the life of your friend to draw and convince him of his need for Christ.

RESPONSE 4: I'VE BEEN BAPTIZED

I can't tell you the number of times I've heard some form of this statement. This response comes in a lot of different ways. Someone may claim that he is saved because he "joined the church" when he was a child. Perhaps he has "walked the aisle" or "prayed the prayer." Some believe they have salvation because they participated in sacraments or went through confirmation. Regardless of how this statement is phrased, the message behind the words is the same: "I'm saved because I *did* something."

There are countless folks in today's church culture who are banking on getting to heaven and receiving eternal life precisely because they feel like they have jumped through the correct spiritual hoops, resulting in their being owed salvation. There are a couple of huge problems with this line of thinking, however.

First of all, Scripture makes it very clear that we are not saved by anything we do! If you remember back to our chapter on prayer, you will recall that Jesus claimed that no one could come to Him unless he was so drawn by the Father. Not only that, but people remain spiritually blind to their sin and need for Christ's gift of salvation unless God gives them the spiritual sight they need to realize these truths. You see, without God making the first move, it would be utterly impossible for any of us to come to Him at all. There is not a single person who has ever lived who just decided one day of his own accord to give God a try! God is the initiator of every relationship.

God is not only the initiator of relationships, He is also the enabler of any salvation experience. Obviously, He has done the work through Christ to make salvation available but that is not where His work ends. According to Ephesians 2:8-9, it is "by grace you are saved through faith, and this is not from yourselves; it is God's gift - not from works, so that no one can boast." God's grace is poured out on us as we exercise faith in Christ's redemptive work. Notice, however, an interesting thing about the faith that we exercise. According to this passage, the faith itself is a gift from God. The faith that you and I put to use in calling on Jesus is not something that we muster up on our own! It is a gift that is given to us by the Holy Spirit of God to enable us to believe and receive the grace that God so richly offers! If the faith were mine, I would have some role to play in my own salvation. I would be able to say, "Hey, look here! My faith was strong enough to save me!" God won't allow that, though. He is the provider of salvation and of the faith required to procure that salvation.

Notice also that no work is involved in this process. When I call out in faith asking Christ to save me, it's as if I were drowning in a sea of sin. The story of Peter walking out to meet Jesus on the waves is a perfect illustration for this. At the point that Peter realized his ability wasn't enough to bear him to Jesus, he called out to the Master who reached out His hand to save him. Drowning in a sea of sin, you and I don't stroke our way to Jesus. We don't build our own raft and float to Jesus. The only rescue available to us comes as we helplessly cry out to Him for salvation, and every time He faithfully provides that which we need.

You and I do no work to initiate a relationship with God. Rather we allow Him to do His work. Nor do we participate in any way in our own rescue. Christ alone provides us with the faith we need to trust in His redemptive work. To take things a step further, we don't really have any power in ourselves to live a life of holiness after coming to Christ. It is Jesus who, through His continuing work in us, changes us into His likeness as we remain surrendered to Him and open to His molding and shaping. Paul put it this way in his letter to the Philippians, "I am sure of this, that He who started a good work in you will carry it on to completion until the day of Christ Jesus."[lxii] His work begins in us as He draws us and calls us to Himself, but His work is not complete until we stand before Him in eternity! You see, the life of the Christian isn't nearly as much about "working" as it is about being "worked-on." You and I do nothing in order to be saved; we simply surrender to Christ as our Lord and Savior. Furthermore, we do little to grow into His likeness. Instead, we continue to surrender to His Lordship as He works in and through us.

All of this is to say that anytime others says they have done something in order to "earn" or "claim" their salvation, they demonstrate a faulty knowledge of the Biblical concept of grace. Being baptized has never saved anyone. We participate in baptism because we have been saved. Walking an aisle or joining a church never saved anyone. We do those things in response to what Christ is doing in us. Praying just the right words never guaranteed anyone's salvation. I don't base my salvation on a prayer that I prayed over thirty years ago but on the promises of the God whom I prayed to this morning as I continue in the relationship into which He drew me. No one is saved because he gives money to the church or provides any service to God. Truth be told, our self-righteousness is trash to God.[lxiii] You and I are only made right before God as we receive the grace He offers by the faith He provides and as we remain rooted in Him through submission and obedience to His ongoing work in us.

If your friend offers this response, your first priority should be to clearly understand what he means. Some of the folks who have shared responses like this with me over the years didn't really believe that their works saved them. Rather, they had never been challenged to think through their salvation experiences in a way that was communicable. As we continued to talk, it sometimes became apparent to me that these people really had experienced true salvation but didn't know how to put that into words. If this turns out to be the case for your friends, rejoice that they are a brother or sister-in-Christ and continue your spiritual conversations in an effort to assist them in accurately framing their salvation stories in the true light of the gospel.

On the other hand, if it becomes apparent that your friend really does believe that salvation is owed to him because of something he has done then remind him that the debt of his sin is so great that there is no action he could possibly take to offset it. We are all spiritually bankrupt before God. Our debt is not something we can work off. The only thing that can fix our hopeless situation is a complete bail-out! That's what Jesus offers.

Let me take a few more moments to elaborate on one aspect of this issue. As already stated, it has become common practice for well-meaning Christians to lead others to pray a "repeat after me" prayer for salvation. These prayers usually center around the three biblical concepts of admitting one's sin and asking for forgiveness, confessing one's need of salvation to God, and expressing belief in Christ's death, burial, and resurrection. Let me be clear that though I believe leading someone to pray a more personal prayer is the best approach, I don't see anything morally wrong with leading people to pray to Christ in this way. I have already pointed out some weaknesses I see in "repeat after me" prayers and would focus for just a moment more on a potentially dangerous pitfall that could be created by leading someone in this way. Through the years, some folks have focused more on the power of this prayer for salvation than the relationship this prayer is intended to recognize. In other words, if we are not careful, it is possible for us to put too much emphasis on the prayer while ignoring the fact that there is no salvation apart from an ongoing, dynamic relationship with the one we are praying to.

If you were to ask me how I know that I'm married, I would definitely point out a few things to prove the fact to you. I would probably reference my wedding day and may recall the vows my wife and I took on that day. These vows are important, much like the salvation prayer, but they are not the *real* proof of my relationship with my wife. I could show you my ring, noting that in the twenty-plus years I've been married I've never taken it off. However, while the ring is a symbol of my marriage, it is not *real* proof of my relationship with my wife. You see, if I wanted to give you solid evidence of my relationship with my wife, the best thing I could do is actually introduce you to her. I would share all about the relationship I have with her now! The fact is that my relationship with Wendy is not based on a bunch of vows that we uttered to one another a couple of decades ago. Rather the relationship is grounded in the reality of our ongoing commitment, loyalty, and love. I have a relationship with her now!

The same is true of a relationship with Jesus. Those who have a true, saving relationship with Christ don't base that relationship on a prayer prayed at some time in the past. Instead, they base it on the ongoing commitment, loyalty, and love that they share with Him on a daily basis. If you ask me how I know I'm saved, I will not tell you that it is because I prayed to Christ thirty-something years ago. I will tell you that it is because I prayed to Him this morning, and He spoke to me through His word and by His Spirit. Was that initial prayer important? Absolutely, but only because it was the starting point of something much greater. Did He save me when that initial prayer was made? Yes, but just as importantly, He is continuing the work of salvation in me today, and ultimately He will be the one to bring my salvation experience to completion in glory!

Hopefully, as you talk to your friend, he will realize that works are of no use when it comes to true salvation. Our only hope is to throw ourselves on the mercies of Christ. If your friend comes to that realization then encourage him to pray to Christ, surrendering himself to Jesus as he calls out to Him for salvation. Make it clear that his prayer, however, is not a work! Rather, it is a request for Christ to do His work in him! If your friend is not ready to call on Jesus, continue to pray for him and look for more opportunities to engage in conversation, knowing that God is faithful to continue drawing him and opening his eyes to his need for Christ's gift of grace.

RESPONSE 5: I THINK THERE'S ANOTHER WAY

We've already discussed the climate of moral relativism that exists in our culture today. Tolerance and equality seem to be the proper and popular terminology that rule every relationship. In a society where equality of ideas is held at a level approaching worship, to claim that one way of thinking exists in exclusivity to others comes across as intolerant and elitist. It's precisely into this mix of ideas that biblical truth claims absolute superiority.

Religious pluralism has come to be espoused by many a celebrity and quite a few politicians in this day and age. These share the belief that it doesn't really matter what one believes so long as one is faithful to his own convictions while avoiding at all costs strong disagreement with those of others. One illustration of this concept which has been used quite often is that of a wagon wheel. According to this theory, heaven and God are represented by the hub at the center of the wheel. People exist along the outer rim of the wheel with a desire to reach the center. The spokes of the wheel represent the different religions in this world, each providing its own definition of morality and a pathway to God. In order for this wheel to remain balanced, it must be recognized by all that no one spoke is greater than the other. Religion, after all, is simply a psychological and social construct meant to provide meaning, purpose, and direction to the lives of adherents.

This is the cultural soup that most people find themselves steeped in. When Christians speak into this atmosphere with a message of absolute truth, exclusive claims about God, and a "repent or perish" message, they are not fondly accepted nor appreciated. The problem is that regardless of attempts to make it fit within a relativistic society, Christianity is by definition different! Think about the differences between Christianity and most of the other world religions. While the rest of the world claims, "earn salvation," Christianity screams, "receive salvation." As the rest of the world speaks of the inherent good of mankind, Christianity proclaims that we are all evil to the core. While the world encourages us to save ourselves, Christianity implores us to cry out for rescue. While the world says build your life, Christianity instructs us to lose our lives so that we may find them in Christ. The world says that you control your destiny, while Christianity claims that your destiny is in God's hands. Finally, most importantly, the world says you can choose your way to heaven, while Christ says, "I, alone, am the way, the truth, and the life."[lxiv]

Make sure that you catch that last part for sure. Many people believe that Jesus is "a way" to eternal life; however, Christ made it clear that He is "the way," the only way, in fact, to eternal life. There is no way under heaven by which men can be saved other than Jesus Christ![lxv] Jesus was one of the most exclusive folks you could ever meet. He had no tolerance for religious pluralism or hypocrisy. Note some of the things He had to say about Himself.

- Jesus claimed to be sinless. "Who among you can convict Me of sin? If I tell the truth, why don't you believe Me? The one who is from God listens to God's words. This is why you don't listen, because you are not from God" (John 8:46-47).
- Jesus claimed to exist eternally with God. "Now, Father, glorify Me in Your presence with that glory I had with You before the world existed" (John 17:5).
- Jesus claimed to be the heavenly king. "'My kingdom is not of this world,' said Jesus. 'If My kingdom were of this world My servants would fight so that I wouldn't be handed over to the Jews. As it is, My kingdom does not have its origin here.' 'You are a king then?' Pilate asked. 'You say that I'm a king,' Jesus replied. 'I was born for this, and I have come into the world for this: to testify to the truth. Everyone who is of the truth listens to My voice'" (John 18:36-37).
- Jesus claims the ability to forgive sin. "'Then He said to her, "Your sins are forgiven. ' Those who were at the table with Him began to say among themselves, 'Who is this man who even forgives sins?'" (Luke 7:48-49).
- Jesus claimed to be able to give eternal life. "'I give them eternal life, and they will never perish—ever! No one will snatch them out of My hand. My Father, who has given them to Me, is greater than all. No one is able to snatch them out of the Father's hand'" (John 10:28-29).
- Jesus claimed to be God. "The Father and I are one" (John 10:30).
- Jesus claimed to be the one and only way to eternal life. "I am the way, the truth, and the life. No one comes to the Father except through Me" (John 14:6).

Jesus left no doubt in the minds of the folks who heard His words that He was anything other than the Son of God sent by the Father to make atonement for the sins of mankind! While some in today's world would love to label Jesus as just another prophet, moral authority, or religious leader, He left absolutely no room for such attempts. Jesus actually made so many exclusive claims about Himself that, if these claims are untrue then we are left with no room to label Him as good or moral. There can be only two alternatives when it comes to Jesus: either He is a liar, and that on the level of a raving lunatic, or He really is the Lord!

In his book *Mere Christianity,* C.S. Lewis makes the following statement, "A man who was merely a man and said the sort of things Jesus said would not be a great moral teacher. He would either be a lunatic—on a level with the man who says he is a poached egg—or else he would be the Devil of Hell. You must make your choice…. You can shut Him up for a fool, you can spit at Him and kill Him as a demon; or you can fall at His feet and call Him Lord and God."[lxvi] Jesus leaves absolutely no room for neutrality among those who would consider Him. Simply stated, either Jesus told the truth about Himself or He was a fraud.

Here is the crux of the situation for our unbelieving friend: a decision must be made about Jesus! And make no mistake about it, every person does make just such a decision. To say that Jesus is just "a way" to God is to call Him a liar. To claim that it is possible to get to heaven on one's own merit is to negate His purpose for coming, thus making Him out to be a lunatic. To put off a decision to follow Him is to thumb one's nose in the face of His mercy, disregarding His divine authority and supreme sacrifice. To hold any opinion of Christ, other than that of Him as Lord and Savior, is to deny the truth of the very claims He made about Himself. The only proper response to Jesus is to recognize Him for who He is, to accept His exclusive claims to be the unique and original truth He meant for them to be, and to surrender to His supreme lordship.

As you discuss this topic with your loved one, point out some of the specific claims that Jesus made about Himself. Ask your friend how these things could be true of Jesus if He was just one of many ways for us to find eternal life. Remind him that regardless of what he believes about Christians as a group, he must still make a decision about Jesus. Point out that tolerance and religious pluralism are primarily truth issues. The decision that must be made by each person is whether or not he believes that Jesus told the truth. If Jesus did tell the truth, then all of this nonsense about different roads leading to heaven is nothing more than fairy tales. State that it is logically impossible for everyone to be right. While riding the fence on issues of faith may be the expected response of the day, it will prove woefully inadequate in eternity.

As you pray and discuss, hopefully your friend will come to see that the idea of all truth being equal doesn't stand up under scrutiny. If this is the case, ask him again if he'd like to place his faith in Christ in light of the truth of the gospel. As always, if the conversation gravitates towards arguing then move on to another subject. Don't burn bridges, but do your best to leave the door open for talking about this issue in the future. Bring it up again as opportunities arise. Remember to pray for your friend, asking that God would grant him an understanding that His truth is the only real truth.

CONCLUSION

While these responses do not give answers to *every* issue that might be brought up in a conversation, they do provide a framework for you to begin to think through how you might talk with others on issues of faith. I believe that much of the pushback you may receive as you talk to folks about your spiritual story will be represented by one of these possible responses. Of course, it is impossible to provide all of the answers to these issues in one chapter. Hopefully, by thinking through these responses, the gears of your mind have begun turning. Continue to think and look for more answers. There are hundreds of Christian books and webpages dedicated to apologetics issues available to you and your friends out there today.[lxvii]

One effective tool I have often used in preparing to talk with others is to play out mock conversations in my head. I try to imagine every direction that a discussion could take and think through every objection a friend might have. If something comes to mind that I myself can't clearly provide an answer for, I do some research or find answers in Scripture. Not only do I think about conversations yet to come, I constantly replay interactions I have already had with people over again in my mind to discover if there was something I could have said differently or to clarify the positions held by others. I have found that this practice provides me with a bit more confidence as I talk with my friends. I have often found that the real conversation will take many of the same twists and turns as the scenario I laid out in my own mind.

One thing I would remind you of is the importance of prayer for this whole approach. Remember that you are asking God to take the lead role in these spiritual conversations. In many ways, that takes the pressure off you to try to make something happen. Recall that we previously stated that God's power is most often preceded by fervent prayer. This entire approach begins with prayer and must be bathed in prayer throughout. The moment you start relying on your own ability will prove to be the point where you place yourself in the driver's seat and may soon find the conversation becoming difficult or worse.

Be careful not to view objections as a purely negative things. You may be challenging your loved one to think about spiritual issues in ways he has never done so. Anytime a person's worldview is challenged there are going to be objections and questions. If your friend is willing to discuss these with you, recognize this as a positive and productive part of this adventure. Have faith that as you explore these issues together you'll be afforded a front row seat to the power and work of God.

One more word of encouragement. Regardless of the direction that these conversations take or the response from your friend, know that you have been faithful to fulfill your role in sharing the greatest gift ever given. One thing I assure you: if you are faithful to share, you can trust and know that some will believe! While everyone you share with may not make a decision to follow Christ, some will! Even for those who don't, you've at least provided an opportunity for them to hear and respond to the truth of the gospel. Be encouraged! God will reward your obedience as you join Him in what He's doing in this world!

Last Things Last

I've shared with you my desire to offer a viable *approach* to relational evangelism rather than a *presentation*. I am confident that this material has provided you with some useful tools for the evangelistic mission we've been given. I pray you've been challenged to accept your responsibility to pray for the lost, encourage other believers to share, and to be obedient yourself in reaching out to others.

It is a sad truth that there are those in our churches who have been believers for years, even decades, yet they have never really shared their faith with anyone. After years in ministry, I realize that we have unintentionally created a church climate that encourages lay people to sit back and relax while "professional Christians" do all the work. The average church member has come to understand church to be a dining room where they are fed rather than a kitchen where they are taught how to feed a hungry world outside the church's walls. This flawed understanding has led to stunted physical growth and spiritual immaturity in a vast number of churches. While poor leadership creates a dependent church culture, productive leaders equip others for the work of evangelism, encourage them to stay the course, and empower them to do the job. I am blessed beyond measure to have served on staff with great men of God who did this very thing! These men taught me what it means to truly lead others to be Great Commission Christians.

There is no backing down from the job of evangelism for the faithful follower. Biblically, we've been commanded. Jesus made it clear that the one responsibility He left with His followers was to carry on the work that He'd been sent to do. While the purpose of Jesus' coming was to make salvation and redemption available to mankind, He left His church here to make that gift accessible to all people in all places. It would have been quite easy for Christ to spirit away His church during or after His ascension, yet He left us behind to represent Him before all people knowing that many would exercise saving faith. There is great incentive for us to accomplish this work as eternal destruction awaits those who die apart from Christ. While the enemy would incite us to be silent, Christ's Spirit implores us to go, to share the gift of His grace, to seek, and to save…just as Jesus has done for us! And we have the promise that if we will be faithful, we will enjoy success! If we will share, some will believe!

Realizing that we are simply carrying on a work that Christ has already begun should set our hearts at ease. Christ has a vested interest in seeing our labor for His kingdom bear fruit. Our first step in joining Him is to see our hearts and the hearts of others prepared for the work He would like to do. Believing that prayer precedes the powerful work of God, faithful followers of Christ make praying for the lost a daily commitment. As we do so, we join our hearts to that of the Father and find that He provides us with passion for the task.

In today's church culture, a relational approach to sharing one's faith seems like a novel idea even though it is exactly how the first Christians went about reaching their friends and neighbors. Their faith was part of who they were, not just a set of facts they wished to present to others for their acceptance. We've placed such a high emphasis on acquisition of knowledge that our understanding of the very nature of faith itself has become flawed. In many ways, we expect people to "believe" in Jesus the same way that they "believe" in George Washington. Therefore, we present facts, logic, and outlines hoping that if people have all the information, they will make a judicious decision about the truth of the message. The problem with this way of thinking is that Biblical belief involves more than just the acknowledgment of facts. It is predicated, rather, on the basis of relationship. In other words, it's not enough to just know *about* Jesus. True salvation requires that we *know* Jesus and, more importantly, that He knows us. While a transfer of knowledge requires little in the way of intimacy to be successful, guiding someone to make an eternally life-altering decision requires much.

I have demonstrated that the best possible way to leverage relationships in spreading the gospel is through the vehicle of conversation. Engaging in conversations rather than presentations removes much of the angst associated with sharing one's faith. This tool allows us to approach each situation from a unique perspective and provides the fluidity needed to meet individuals where they are with the message of Christ. While what I've shared with you may seem at times to be just another presentation, I assure you that it is not. With this approach, you are incorporating prayer as the preparatory tool it was meant to be, asking questions to gain a feel for where other people are spiritually, sharing answers from God's Word, and encouraging folks to take a step of faith.

The beauty of this approach is that you only make use of the portions of this material that God leads you to use and gives you opportunity for. As long as you're praying for lost people on a daily basis, the specific words aren't that important. If you leave a question out, it's no big deal. If your conversations get interrupted, have no worries. The only portion that is indispensable is biblical, and even for that you do little more than facilitate an interaction between your friend and God's Word. I hope that thinking about evangelism in this way moves you past simple obedience to sharing with excitement. I pray that you will gain a passion for sharing your faith that perhaps you've never had before. You see, I believe that as you are obedient to do your part, you will see amazing results as God demonstrates His power and willingness to work in and through you!

THE CHALLENGE

I want to leave you with a very real challenge. Each of us knows at least five individuals whose relationships with Christ we are unsure of. Can I ask you to dream with me for a minute?

What if you began praying for your five by name on a daily basis? What if you prayed that God would specifically draw your friends to Himself? What if you prayed that God would surround them with Christians who are enthusiastic about sharing their faith? What if you prayed for God appointed teachable moments to happen in the lives of each? What if you prayed that God would prepare you with just the right words when those moments occur? What if you prayed that your friends' eyes would be open to their inescapable need for Jesus?

How would things change for your friends and loved ones if you were to make spiritual conversations a common occurrence? Would their chances of believing increase if you were to be as free to talk about spiritual things as you are to talk about sports, shopping, or television? What if you made it a priority to use conversations to gauge where your friends are spiritually and to create open doors for discussing more intimate faith issues? What if, at the proper time, you presented the foundational truths of your faith by way of God's Word? What if you leveraged every part of your relationships to introduce your loved ones to the one with whom you have the greatest and most important relationship? What if your heart ached for them to come to know Christ as you do? What if you chose today to begin to make intentional spiritual investments in the lives of others in the hopes that they would come to Christ? All of this may seem like a big step, but I assure you it's not. Start off small and go from there. Start with prayer and wait expectantly for God to begin to work things out.

So, who are your 5? Could 5 souls be changed for eternity because of you? I say, "Yes!"

MY 5

_____

_____

_____

_____

_____

Well, what are you waiting for? Eternity starts now!!

> *"Everyone who calls on the name of the Lord will be saved. But how can they call on Him in whom they have not believed? And how can they believe without hearing about Him? And how can they hear without a preacher? And how can they preach unless they are sent? As it is written: How welcome are the feet of those who announce the gospel of good things!"*

> Romans 10:13-15

Endnotes

i   http://www.barna.org/barnaupdate/faith-spirituality/648-is-evangelism-going-out-of-style#.VJMmx8am38s

ii   Romans 10:14-15

iii   Hebrews 11:6

iv   http://public.imb.org/globalresearch/Pages/default.aspx

v   Romans 10:15b

vi   Mark 15:15-16

vii   John 20:21

viii   Acts 1:8

ix   Luke 16:19-31

x   Mark 9:43-44

xi   Romans 3:10-12

xii   2 Peter 3:9

xiii   John 14:6, bracketed text is mine

xiv   Matthew 7:21-23

xv   Romans 5:8

xvi   Genesis 3

xvii   John 3:16-18

xviii   John 1:12-13

xix   www.godandscience.org/apologetics/smj.pdf

xx   John 6:43-44a

xxi   John 6:64-65

xxii   Matthew 9:37-38

xxiii   1 Peter 3:15

xxiv   Colossians 4:2-4

xxv   Ephesians 6:19-20

xxvi   Isaiah 55:11

xxvii   2 Corinthians 4:3-4

xxviii Ephesians 1:17-19

xxix Pew Research Center, Pew Forum's U.S. Religious Landscape Survey, 2007, http://religions.pewforum.org/reports

xxx Pew Research Center, 2010, http://www.pewforum.org/2010/02/17/religion-among-the-millennials/

xxxi John 14:6

xxxii Pew Research Center, 2012. http://www.pewresearch.org/fact-tank/2013/10/23/5-facts-about-atheists/

xxxiii Luke 22:69; Acts 2:32-36, 7:55-56; Romans 8:34; Ephesians 1:20; Colossians 3:1; Hebrews 1:3, 8:1, 10:12, 12:2, 1 Peter 3:22

xxxiv Isaiah 56:10-11

xxxv Hebrews 4:12

xxxvi Matthew 13:1-23

xxxvii Isaiah 55:11

xxxviii James 1:17

xxxix James 1:17; Numbers 23:19; Psalm 102:27; Habakkuk 1:12

xl Romans 5:12-19

xli 1 Corinthians 5:21

xlii Romans 4:25

xliii 1 John 4:10

xliv http://www.merriam-webster.com/dictionary/lord

xlv Matthew 28:18

xlvi Philippians 2:10-11

xlvii Matthew 16:24

xlviii 1 Corinthians 15:12-19

xlix John 12:25

l Hebrews 4:12

li 2 Peter 3:9

lii Matthew 5:16

liii Packer, J. I., *Knowing God* (Downers Grove: Intervarsity Press, 1993), 110.

liv John 4

lv 2 Timothy 3:16-17

lvi Luke 12:20-21

lvii Luke 16:19-31

lviii 2 Corinthians 6:1-2

lix Hebrews 3:15, 4:1

lx Matthew 11:30

lxi Hebrews 13:8

lxii Philippians 1:6

lxiii Isaiah 64:6

lxiv John 14:6

lxv Acts 4:12

lxvi Lewis, C.S., *Mere Christianity* (New York: Harper Collins, 2001), 52.

lxvii Visit truelife.org for many more answers to tough questions

21784249R00105

Printed in Great Britain
by Amazon